LOVE AND SOUL-MAKING

Searching The Depths of Romantic Love

BY
STACEY SHELBY, Ph.D.

CHIRON PUBLICATIONS • ASHEVILLE, NORTH CAROLINA

www.ChironPublications.com

Interior and cover design by Danijela Mijailovic
Printed primarily in the United States of America.

ISBN 978-1-68503-039-1 paperback
ISBN 978-1-68503-040-7 hardcover
ISBN 978-1-68503-041-4 electronic
ISBN 978-1-68503-042-1 limited edition paperback

Library of Congress Cataloging-in-Publication Data Pending

Foreword

In *Love and Soul-Making*, Dr. Stacey Shelby articulates with care and depth the relationship between love and soul—as particularly told in the myth of Eros and Psyche. But she doesn't simply recount the myth and restate what has been told before. She dreams the myth onwards as C. G. Jung instructed. Shelby judiciously presents how love and soul have traditionally been conceptualized in depth psychology, and then tests this against the bar of ongoing human experience—showing how those pricked by Eros' arrow and captured by Psyche's beauty have continued to re-imagine their relationship. The result, then, is not just a retelling of ideas, but an evocation of what it feels like to love soul, and to make soul from love—from its ecstasy and pain, its pathology and divinity.

In the process, Shelby reveals how Eros and Psyche show up in human relationships, in romance, in idealizations and projections. But more importantly, she sees through these literal enactments as James Hillman described, to disclose the deeper significance of Eros and Psyche, their archetypal significance for every individual—regardless of relationship status. As Shelby brilliantly and convincingly argues, romance is first and foremost about the individual's calling to love soul, their own soul, and the soul of the world, and reciprocally to find soul in, to make soul from, and to serve soul through love's many expressions. *Love and Soul-*

Making itself exemplifies this love and calling—embodying the soul Shelby has made from her life and experiences.

Dylan Hoffman, Ph.D.
Adjunct Faculty—Pacifica Graduate Institute
M.A./Ph.D. Depth Psychology—Jungian & Archetypal Studies

Table of Contents

For the love of soul

Chapter 1
Love and Soul: Invocation

Romantic love is the ultimate transformer. It enthrals with a sip of love potion or enchants with the prick of Eros' arrow. Who can resist? But as romance unfolds, we are enticed into greater awareness of self and other—sometimes through a crisis that ensues. The only way through is one tentative step in front of the other. The old idealized life dies away and a new life gestates quietly. With each step, we are invited to look into our deepest recesses, to discover what we didn't even know existed. Each revelation is a mirror and a glimpse of our own soul. We come to marvel at the person we are getting to know, the one who is looking back at us with a new gaze—and who is giving us a new view of ourselves. Something within us doesn't follow societal rules, but has its own, which are only revealed to us a bit at a time. This 'Other' within us challenges us and brings out the best and worst in us—our fullness. She is Psyche, the human soul. She pursues what she loves, which is beyond all logos and rational safety. Psyche follows Eros, who is the immortal god of love. He is Love as the sacred connecting principle. We encounter these two most poignantly in the arena of romantic love. As we walk with them, we get to know paradox, including the paradox of knowing sacred, divine love through the experience of embodied human love. In embracing soul as life's muse, we come into relationship with, indeed we fall in love with, Mystery. In following what we love, we follow soul, and experience enchantment in our own unique and precious life.

Meeting the Swan

Before I started writing this book, I felt an idea gestating in the darkness, a new life. But I felt stuck. We were ten months into the coronavirus pandemic, under intense restrictions of freedoms, and I was engulfed in the deep dark of Canada's winter. One morning, I clearly asked myself, "How will I get unstuck?" As I did, from my window, I saw a lone brilliant white swan in the slough behind my house! I ran outside with a remarkable sense of excitement and urgency. I had to see it closer. It gave a strange honk and kept a wary distance from me. Its grace and size were magnificent. In the dark, rainy days of winter, its brilliant whiteness was stark. I tried to take photos and gazed at it with wonder and awe. Eventually, someone walking a dog came by and I commented, "So strange it is alone." They carried on with barely a notice until the dog alarmed the swan and it flew off. I couldn't believe its wing-span! The swan impressed me so much that I had to research why it would be alone.

I came across a few initial myths and facts. They typically do mate for life, but on rare occasion will change or lose partners, and then usually seek out a new partner. As a totem animal, harkening to the ugly duckling tale, they are symbolic of transformation and the realization of our true beauty and grace. Further, they are associated with romantic love; the image of two swans with their necks entwined or forming a heart-shape often represents love. The swan immediately became the totem of this work—both in regard to transformation and romantic love. The premise that romantic love leads to the transformation that causes us to realize our true beauty and grace is the guiding star of this work. The swan embodies all of this and is the perfect synchronistic gift and blessing that landed in the slough outside my window and lifted me out of the slough I was stuck within. I'm left with the question: How do swans find a new mate?

Writing this work on romantic love as a vessel of alchemical transformation has made me wrestle with an imposter complex. I have been unpartnered—at least in the traditional sense—for 12 years at the time of this writing. "Who am I to write about romantic love as the vessel for spiritual transformation leading to ones' innate beauty?" I have previously been critical of other Jungian writers exploring the topic of romantic love (even though I understood and deeply admired their works), because they too were unpartnered in the traditional sense for most of their lives as well. So, what perspective might writers like myself have to bring to this exploration? In the spirit of alchemy, I have to move towards that which I want to push away, the imposter complex. In moving towards it, I find the perspective I need. Psyche and Eros are not solely expressed in external romance. As archetypal figures and powers, they are always inherently at work within. The soul of love and the love of soul are expressed primarily in our relationship with ourselves. The magnum opus of Psyche's union with Eros is foremost an inner work. In fact, when we read the myth of romance in the West with double-vision, we can see both the literal and the metaphorical—we can perceive the Otherworldliness at the same time as we perceive the sensate world. So, I do not need a literal, human partner to undertake what is ultimately an alchemical transmutation. From this perspective, I set out to approach this work as the alchemists did, in an imaginal manner and symbolically, and with a great deal of uncertainty stepping towards the unknown. I gathered the energy to begin from the swan and the idea that this would be an inward exploration—except for the experience of synchronicity or outward mirroring. Paradoxically, all this inner focus is for the

3

purpose of living a meaningful, joyful life imbued with romance—both inwardly and outwardly.

I tried to assure myself and my imposter complex with the story of Chiron, the wounded healer, who could never heal himself, but could teach others the healing arts, including Asclepius. In Chiron's effort to heal himself, he did master medicine and shared that wisdom. As a clinical therapist, I have the privilege of being invited to bear witness to peoples' trials and tribulations involving love. Perhaps some of us that do not have the same kind of lived experience, but bear their own yearning and longing and hold space for the yearning and longing of others, can have something of objective value to offer. I have been wounded by love—perhaps an irreparable wound—but in my effort to heal it, maybe my inner archetype of Chiron has afforded me a useful perspective to share with others.

I share all this because I want to be transparent about my initial resistance to writing this book. It does, after all, require a lot of discipline to write a book, and demands the sacrifice of other things I enjoy. Gradually, I began to get to know the material as I showed up for "writing dates" to see what might happen. Over time, I began to enjoy these writing dates with a certain amount of wonder at where it was going. Then, after a few months, I was pricked by Eros' arrow and had fallen in love with the book that was revealing itself to me word by word. About that time—once I felt engrossed by the book—I had a dream of the masculine giving birth to a baby girl: *I am with a very pregnant man, I seem to support him in some entrusted capacity. He tells me the name of his soon-to-be born daughter (the name I forget upon waking); it is all unfathomable to me that he is pregnant. His ex-wife, with whom he shares two adult children, is the egg donor, though she will not be a parent to this child. He wanted to parent this child and felt she was the best person to donate the egg. Then his*

4

water broke (I am mystified, but it happened)! He has a close male friend who is present as well, and the two of us will take him to the hospital for delivery.

Then the next night, I dreamt: *The man has gone to work and I am caring for the new born girl. We are in a warehouse type space, not as nice as an industrial loft. I snuggle the little girl, but she is growing quickly and even though in chronological time she was just born, she is about six-seven months developmentally. She needs more sustenance than breast milk, which the ex-wife was absently supplying through pumping. I asked my mother, who was there, to "run to the store and pick up some organic brown rice cereal" that I could mix with the breast milk for the baby to start introducing solids. While my mother is gone, I cuddle the newborn and enjoy the oxytocin-snuggles. Then a courier arrives and delivers two love seats. I sign for them, but then realize the delivery is incomplete. Both love seats are missing the bench attachments, so they can't be assembled. I'll have to contact the furniture company to sort it out and I hope that I have not made a mistake by signing for the incomplete delivery.*

Then the night progresses until morning, and I awake after a final dream: *The baby girl has just turned one, and the man and I are tidying up after a joyful first birthday party for her. There is a feeling of elation and we joke about looking forward to her second birthday party. There is an understanding and acceptance that her accelerated development and aging is outside of chronological time.*

What was unfolding in my life at the time of these dreams? Prior to really falling in love with this book, I was working on writing the *Alchemy of Love* (a working title for another book in development) and I was getting bogged down and stuck as I felt it needed to be about love in all of its expressions—rather than exclusively romantic love. The two love seats inspired the idea to write two books on different aspects of love: romantic and the other types of love. Appropriately, in the beginning there is something about them being incomplete due to an "attachment" piece missing. I wasn't emotionally attached to writing two books at all, as it seemed like a daunting task given all the other responsibilities in my life. Nevertheless, the oxytocin from cuddling the baby girl (this book: *Love and Soul-Making*) is the attachment hormone; therefore, time with her—with the writing work—seems to create the necessary attachment. The pregnant man as a symbol is profound. At risk of oversimplification, he was something of a king and represented a new type of masculinity giving birth to a girl child. My dream ego, my conscious position, was as a support to the masculine aspect. He seems to represent a mature masculinity that wants to be of service and support to the feminine as represented in the girl. Also, he is the active aspect that I rely on to bring my work and voice into the world, so it is appropriate that he is at work. The girl child reminded me of the birth of Pleasure or Harmonia, who is born from the final union of Psyche and Eros. Indeed, in my life, I had been enjoying a new state of joy and, in particular, feminine expression. For instance, I was wearing pink blouses and ruffles, which are something I would historically have shunned in favor of denim and a leather jacket—having grown up as a rocker in the 80s. Yet, this new expression of femininity brought me an unexpected amount of joy and pleasure in my attitude throughout the day. I felt lighter and buoyant. It is also worth noting the "man" in the dream is something of a hermaphrodite in that he is able to create life and give birth to it. The last time I had dreams of hermaphroditic figures was when I was writing *Tracking the Wild Woman*.

With these synchronicities, the symbol of the swan, and dreams guiding and enlivening the path, we begin our journey of love *and* soul-making, love *of* soul, and towards the birth of Pleasure.

Explorations of Psyche and Eros

In each chapter, we will explore Psyche and Eros and include select perspectives from other depth psychology writers to help us navigate. We begin with the myth of Psyche and Eros; and will rely on this tale as a path to love of soul. This book has developed from the graduate course I teach on the same topic at Pacifica Graduate Institute, in Santa Barbara, California. The content includes a curated selection of Jungian authors designed to offer various perspectives and invoke your own perspective that will hopefully lead to your unique inquiry into love (Eros) and soul (Psyche). As we go through the chapters in this book, I'll offer my thoughts, synthesize in my words, and highlight other authors. The process of reading this book is meant to be psychoactive and interactive for the reader as it weaves its way toward the alchemical gold: the love of soul and the birth of pleasure.

Also, every chapter includes Reflection Questions and Active Imagination Questions and Answers. The "Reflection Questions" are for you, the reader, to contemplate and journal about. Journaling helps us connect to the quiet inner world and hear soul's tender voice. The Active Imagination Q & A allows for a broader range of responses to inspire the reader, and affords me the creative license to flesh out ideas in dialogue and illustrate the wisdom at work in the imaginal. True to psyche's preference for polyvalence, this approach allows for multiple perspectives and ideas to be explored and shared beyond the monovalence of my conscious perspective.

Finally, in many of the chapters, I have included additional exercises for the reader to engage with: a projection exercise; working with Psyche's four tasks; and a beauty exercise. These six exercises are designed to open up the material for the reader. I encourage these be done through journaling and ideally with a therapist or trusted friend(s) to share your responses and have them witnessed. I usually facilitate these six exercises in a group workshop format but have adapted it here.

We will start with an introduction to the story of Psyche and Eros and then consider what this myth is about, and why we even look to myth. The story of Psyche and Eros was originally written in the 2nd century C.E. by Lucius Apuleius in a novel called *The Golden Ass*. It's the story of a hero's journey; however, in the middle of the story there's the beautiful little tale of Psyche and Eros, which has come to inspire the imagination of many Jungians and, indeed, is probably the birthplace of the model of romantic love in the West. Myths and fairy tales are important as guides for how archetypes interact with each other within the psyche. As such, we can read it as a symbolic dream. Because it's universal— it comes from the collective unconscious—it doesn't necessarily apply to any particular culture, it represents an archetypal pattern. We can interpret it both on the personal level and the collective level.

As we explore this story, consider the terrain it maps and the guidance it provides. There are varied perspectives available in contemplating myth, my suggestion is to allow all of them to wash over you and see what resonates. In Robert Johnson's view, shared in his 1989 book *She: Understanding Feminine Psychology,* he suggests the story is about understanding feminine psychology in both men and women. Conversely, Marie-Louise von Franz, (1970) in *The Golden Ass of Apuleius: The Liberation of the Feminine in Man*, suggests that, because it's within the context of a larger story that follows the hero's journey, it is about the liberation of the feminine principle in men. Erich Neumann also wrote about it and we'll approach his ideas more toward the end of the book—he's aligned with Robert Johnson in his approach to it as the development of the feminine.

Academically, I identify as a post-Jungian who is trying to liberate myself from these engender terms of feminine and masculine, because they get conflated with woman and man. However, it is very difficult to talk about symbolic things without their personification. My perspective is that the tale is about coming into relationship to soul as Psyche within the human psyche. The human psyche is a mirror of the *anima mundi*, world's soul. I prefer to move away from gender notions as they rapidly become too binary. Furthermore, in the story the connecting principle and god of love, Eros, also evolves, though we don't get to learn much about how that happens—only that he's transformed by the end of the four impossible tasks that Psyche faces.

The tale is an invitation to love soul and in loving soul we find pleasure. The journey often gets enacted through the literalism of romantic love—soul needs the struggles and vitality that is found in romantic love—after all, what Psyche loves is love, Eros. I invite you to distinguish masculine and feminine from particular humans, even though culturally the distinction is often blurred. I will strive to refer to man and woman only when I am talking about humans who identify with those particular genders, and to minimize use of the terms masculine and feminine principles except when I am talking about the symbolic and archetypal. For individuals who are outside of binary gender identification, I invite you to work with the symbolic personification of the principle in whatever image is presented to you. Matters of the heart and soul are most certainly *not* constricted by our limited language around gender. In fact, the closer we move to soul, the more we know of paradox and its myriad perspectives.

Because the lived experience is so central to the process of soulful development through loving, even for those of us who have been unpartnered for extended durations, we will also explore how this myth is a map of the internal stages of the romance between love and soul—depicted in the various experiences that romantic love takes us through. The external lived experience can so often and accurately reflect the development of certain archetypal relationships within our psyches. However, the outward enactment in a particular partnership is a requirement. Having been single a long time, the absence of an external romance has not inhibited my internal engagement with Psyche and Eros. Nevertheless, human romance *can* mediate our encounter with the archetypals. My own past relationship challenges certainly contributed to my personal development and to my creative work such as writing and content creation for courses.

To shed more light on the romance between love and soul, we're also going to analyze the story of Tristan and Iseult. Emerging in the 11th century C.E., it also belongs to the mythology of romantic love in the Western world. It also includes a hero's tale. If we approach the hero's journey as a depiction of developing the ego, it pairs nicely with the development of the soul, whether in men or women. Ego, I would define briefly as an individual's conscious identity—it circumscribes what someone knows about themselves. We want an ego that is both open to the unknown and strong enough to endure the emergence of contents from the unconscious or the archetypal realm, especially as the archetypal starts to present itself to consciousness—so that we don't lose ourselves in it and, therefore, become inflated by identifying with the archetypal, particularly that of the Self.

Also, before moving forward, it's important that I introduce the terms *anima* and *animus*. Classically, anima is the archetype of soul, often personified in feminine figures. The animus is the archetype of spirit, often personified in masculine figures. In contemporary Jungian scholarship, the anima and animus are both viewed as belonging to everyone, not, as Jung initially expressed, to a specific gender. Jung often referred to the anima, soul, as belonging to men, and the animus, spirit, as belonging to women. I suspect that the anima-animus is different expressions of the same archetype that both require development within each person's individual psyche. Their function is to mediate the relationship between the conscious personality, ego, and the unconscious. They are elusive figures that can't be captured by any particular description—which is true for these figures and terms that relate so closely to the Mystery. We run into a challenge in talking and writing about them because they are dynamic, living archetypal expressions that like to defy definition. Even though the conscious mind prefers clarity—and concrete definitions provide that—we have to hold the terms and definitions lightly, less as literally true, and more like mythopoetic, symbolic lens that allow us to be in relationship with, and to learn from these figures.

As noted, the hero's journey, as described by Joseph Campbell, can be a map for the development of the ego through its various stages—including the descent to the underworld, and eventually, the return with the boon. Other myths can be maps for viewing the stages of psychological development that we go through. With the myth of Eros and Psyche—and in particular with the experience of human relationship and human love—we go through stages of psychological development similar to those portrayed in the hero's journey. The similarity is in how this particular myth provides us with a way through our struggles, incited by loving, so that we can return with a boon and with a greater psychological integration of more aspects of the unconscious—in particular the soul. Symbolically we can view Psyche as the development of the human soul. We can also understand Eros as a representative of the development of the connecting principle—even though he is largely absent from the tale. The particular problem with this

11

story, while it does lead to reunification and integration at the conclusion, is that we don't really have much information about what exactly Eros is doing throughout the story. I don't think there is necessarily an answer for this; we can certainly speculate, because we know he's Aphrodite's son and he's doing her bidding in some way. However, when Psyche gives birth to their daughter, Pleasure (one translation of the child's name), we can see new life, or the third thing, being born out of the *coniunctio* of the masculine and feminine aspects.

The triumph of Psyche's love, viewed as her ascension to Olympus, was an event that has profoundly affected Western mankind for 2,000 years. For two millennia, the mysterious phenomenon of romantic love has occupied the centre of psychic development, and of culture, art, and religion. The child born of this union is different than the Hermaphrodite, who doesn't retain two separate identities and becomes merged into one. The unification of two separate individuals who retain their own identities is of higher significance, according to both Jung and Neumann.

Let's review the tale: *Psyche is a such a beautiful human that people start to revere her as more beautiful than the goddess Aphrodite. "Though all admired her divine loveliness, they did so merely as one admires a statue finished to perfection" (Apuleius, para. 33). Aphrodite is offended by this, being the goddess of beauty, love, and sexuality—and seeks to destroy the young Psyche. She commands her reckless and irresponsible son, Eros, to take care of this problem for her, "punish mercilessly, that arrogant beauty" (para. 31). She arranges for Psyche to be wed—although, killed is actually her intention—on top of a mountain. Eros, however, falls in love with the beautiful Psyche on sight by accidently pricking himself with his own arrow. So rather than killing her, Zephyrus, the west wind, carries them away. Eros makes Psyche promise to* never look at him, thus she can never see her beloved except in the cloaked darkness, and he's gone during the day. Psyche lives in joyful, blissful ignorance for a period of time while Eros keeps his identity secret. After a while, the ignorance is no longer blissful, as Psyche's sisters become jealous because they don't like this whole situation and it seems they're the only ones that actually know about it. The sisters "stung by frantic lust and malignant jealousy" (para. 27) plant little seeds of doubt and negativity in Psyche's mind and tell her that Eros must be a horrible dragon monster—since he won't let her see him. Psyche eventually gets confused by these stories and accusations. She decides to hide a lamp in their room, so when Eros falls asleep, she can light it and see the dragon-monster that's in her bed. She prepares the lamp and gets a knife, because she wants to be prepared to slay the monster. That night, she shines the light on his face long enough to see that it's the beautiful face of the god of love, Eros. As she explores his arrows, she accidently pricks herself and falls madly in love with her husband, full of desire for Desire. As she kisses him, a hot drop of oil from the lamp lands on Eros and wakes him. Psyche has violated his plea to never look at him. He feels betrayed, utterly betrayed, and flees. Eros leaves Psyche in despair. She realizes her lover is a beautiful god and is actually not a monster at all.

In her sorrow, Psyche eventually goes to Aphrodite and pleads and begs for Aphrodite's help in winning back the love and confidence of Eros. Aphrodite, meaning to destroy the beautiful Psyche still, sends her to complete four impossible tasks, each one designed to kill Psyche so that she cannot achieve her goal of being with the beautiful Eros. The first task that Aphrodite gives to Psyche is to sort and separate a heap of various grains and seeds by dawn. Now, this an impossible task and Psyche realizes it and collapses in tears, hopeless. "Then there appeared an ant, one of those miniature farmers; grasping the size of the problem," (para.

10). It summoned all the other ants and they take pity on her. They gather and help with the sorting so the task gets completed by morning. Psyche goes back to Aphrodite, who is furious and creates a second impossible task: to collect the wool from very aggressive, dangerous mountain sheep or rams, which is impossible because if she is seen by them they will ram her to death. Again, she feels hopeless and considers just killing herself. This time, a divinely-inspired reed gives Psyche instructions on how to gather the wool "when their rage is calmed and their attention is relaxed, shake the branches of the nearby trees" (para. 13). She is to do this at dusk after the inflammatory heat of the day has subsided. And she is not to take if from the sheep directly. Thus, Psyche manages to complete the second task, again with the intervention of a nature figure. Aphrodite, now really furious, gives her a third impossible task. This task is to collect water from the River Styx—the river of life and death—in a delicate crystal goblet. There are foreboding cliffs and banks with no way to get down to the river and the whole thing is impossible. Psyche again falls into suicidal despair. This time Zeus takes pity on the poor girl and sends his golden eagle that helps her by taking the goblet and dipping it just right, in the right place, and takes just the right amount of water with the crystal goblet. The eagle returns it to Psyche at the river edge, thus completing this third significant and impossible task. Psyche returns to Aphrodite who cannot believe this. She sends Psyche on her fourth and final task that will surely finish her, that's her intention. This task is to journey to the underworld to meet the goddess who presides there, Persephone. Her task is to fetch a casket of Persephone's beauty ointment and bring it back to Aphrodite. Again, Psyche realizes this task means certain death and this time she intends to throw herself off a tower to end her own life. But the tower speaks to her and gives her instructions, detailed instructions, on how to journey to the underworld and how to come back and complete the journey. She must find the track hidden in a trackless country side that leads to the breathing-hole of Dis (Hades) and to the forbidden road that leads to the palace of Orcus. She is instructed to carry in her hands cakes of barley meal, and two coins in her mouth. The tower foretells her: "You will meet a lame donkey with a lame driver . . . He will ask you to hand him some sticks fallen from the load, but you must say nothing and pass by in silence" (para. 18). Next, she will come to the river of Death and its harbourmaster Charon who ferries wayfarers for a cost, which he immediately demands (one of the coins in her mouth for each crossing). As she crosses the sluggish stream, she must not be swayed by pity for an old dead man who swims toward her reaching out and asking for help. Once across the river of Death, the tower warns her she will be met by some old women weavers who will ask her to help—this is yet another ruse inspired by Aphrodite. She must hang-on to her cakes until she gets to the fearsome three-headed dog of Hades. She is to give a cake to the beast for passage in each direction. Finally, she will sit with the goddess of the Underworld who will invite her to a feast. The tower instructs her to "sit on the ground and ask for some coarse bread." Then she can ask for the casket of beauty cream. Upon receiving it, Psyche is instructed to backtrack the way she came. "But this prohibition above all I bid you observe: do not open or look into the box that you bear or pry at all into its hidden store of divine beauty" (para. 19). Psyche does almost all of this, and amazingly well at that: she passes through all the various hurdles, and is returning from the underworld, at which point she breaks her promise to not open the beauty cask. She thinks, "to be carrying divine beauty and not to help myself to even a tiny bit of it, so as perhaps to please my beautiful love" (para 21). Thus, she opens it! Upon opening the casket, she falls into a state of unconsciousness, right at the precipice, as she's about to complete the task. Her *state of complete unconsciousness then arouses Eros—finally, as he has been suffering in anguish in his mother's chamber, healing from his burns—to come to her rescue. Then we have the fairy tale kiss. In rescuing Psyche, he escapes from his mother's tower. Some stories say he awakes her with the kiss, some stories say he pricks her with his arrow. She awakens, and they then bring the beauty ointment to Aphrodite. Aphrodite at this point is satisfied. Eros wants to marry; they have a fantastic wedding with all the Gods and Goddesses, on Mount Olympus. Psyche, whose name means both butterfly and soul in Greek, metamorphosed into a winged goddess. We learn that she's been pregnant during her task and she now gives birth to their daughter, whose name often translates as Pleasure.*

Understanding the various stages and symbols of this rich story, and in particular the four tasks, is valuable in understanding the development of the human soul—psyche, the soul—through the sufferings of love, in particular the sufferings of romantic love. The story shows us the often-experienced stages of romantic love and it also shows us how they play out internally in soul-making. While you are reading this book, engaging with the reflection questions and exercises in the following chapters, allow the story to dance around in your dreams—ideally, you'll write your dreams down too. I invite you to consider your beliefs about romantic love; maybe there are other models of romantic love that you want to be moving toward or exploring, or maybe you want to liberate yourself from this one. Perhaps you want to find a new way to be in this model of romantic love. Keep in mind, romantic love is a way of being in service to soul. The field of depth psychology is in service to soul. Eros is the god of love, so this literally is the story of the relationship between soul and love—that soul wants love, and love wants soul. It's also a story of Aphrodite; we cannot talk about this myth without talking about Aphrodite and the role she plays in sending Psyche on this particular journey of suffering and longing, leading ultimately to the *hieros gamos* between love and soul.

There are two forms of archetypal femininity in the myth of Psyche and Eros. The first is the great goddess Aphrodite, or Venus in Roman mythology. Aphrodite is the goddess of love, beauty, and sexuality and reigns in the unconscious as a result of being born of the sea; "one might as well confront a tidal wave" (Johnson, 1989, p. 3), since she can be so overpowering and unrelatable. And yet, that is precisely Psyche's—the dulcet human soul's—task, to learn to relate to this formidable femininity of the unconscious. Aphrodite carries a mirror, which is, in part, symbolic of how romantic love reveals our projections. In the face of the person we fall in love with, we find unconscious elements of ourselves. To that we must ask, what is being mirrored back? When we see the god or goddess-like qualities in another, it is Aphrodite mirroring back to us our own divinity. Psyche is symbolic of a young, naïve femininity that must reckon with a jealous mother-in-law who seemingly attempts to hinder new growth at every turn. Psyche's mortal beauty is a curse because people don't relate to her on a human level, further it enrages Aphrodite as humans start to worship Psyche rather than the great goddess. It is Psyche's beauty that sets this tale in motion. But, as Psyche perseveres, she then matures until she births a new consciousness. There is a push-pull dynamic where the Aphroditic principle obstructs the development of consciousness. Paradoxically, in doing so, she shows us our unconsciousness by mirroring it back to us, so that we can become more conscious of where we are immature. This impels us psychologically toward soul-making, maturation, and the gestation of new life. The tension between the primordial archetypal feminine and the new innocent feminine can feel like warring principles within the psyche as the person is in the process of birthing a new conscious attitude. Indeed, the work of resolving these inner warring elements can be the work of a life time, but the effort produces the opus, which is your own life.

From the perspective of Marie-Louise von Franz (1970) the Psyche and Eros story is embedded within the larger context of Apuleius' story and thus it is an archetypal dream. This story illustrates the marriage quaternity of a real couple and their corresponding archetypal complements, the anima and animus. In classical Jungian terms, the marriage quaternity is a symbol of wholeness and totality, achieved through the individuation process. Von Franz (1970) wrote, "Love with its passion and pain becomes the urge toward individuation, which is why there is no real process of individuation without the experience of love, for love tortures and purifies the soul" (p. 82). That is the purpose: the gold or gift for the soul tortured by love is individuation. Individuation is a Jungian term I'll quickly define here, but will expand on as we go. It describes something fluid that can't quite be contained, so Jung too offered many different definitions. It can be viewed as the movement towards becoming a whole, indivisible—as in, no longer divided—person. More and more of the opposites and paradoxes become reconciled within one's psyche. Pairs of opposites like the masculine and feminine aspects of the psyche are wed in a *coniunctio*, a union—resulting in an individual's deeper realization of wholeness. Likewise, conscious and unconscious aspects become more integrated as the ego becomes more aware of unconscious forces that are ever-active. The individuation process is this beautiful, struggling movement towards greater and greater wholeness or authenticity— becoming the most natural and innate version of ourselves. We can experience personal growth through the tortures and enchantments of love.

18

The tortures of love and Eros' abonnement by flying off result in the widening of the personality. The process brings more life and more aspects of the personality into activity, and this we can consider psychological healing. Specifically, that means "an access to religious experience, a discovery of the deeper meaning of life and of healing emotions" (von Franz, 1970, p.87). This is done through the ego coming into relationship with the contents of the psyche, that is integration. The relationship is two-way, human ego to archetypal god or goddess, and vice versa. This is the process of incarnating the divine. Initially this process happens before the ego is even aware of it—there is an impetus that arises within consciousness from the god-goddess who wants to incarnate. In writing *Tracking the Wild Woman Archetype*, wild woman was the goddess that wanted to incarnate through me. Thus, by the end of writing that book, I realized that I was not tracking her, but rather she was tracking me all along. That was the moment of integration. Prior to that, "I" (consciousness) was still building a relationship with her. The creative initiative of the process comes from the other side, from the semi-conscious or unconscious archetype. Aphrodite, however, does not like to incarnate in humans, as seen in her rightful jealousy toward Psyche, for it is too narrow for her immortal omnipotence. Nevertheless, she is the archetypal force who has been the catalyst for this book, and frankly, she has taken me to task. This has been done by establishing a conscious relationship with the psyche, thus making room for Aphrodite's archetypal activity, which has been the creative process of writing this book. It has been important to give homage to Aphrodite, even though the book discusses Eros and Psyche; Aphrodite is the patron of this book.

Let's take closer look at Eros in the myth. For the majority of the tale he is absent. From other myths we know he is the son-lover of Aphrodite; his paternal origin story varies. One of the characteristics of myth is that there is not only one story, there are many and often contradictory ones; myth invite us to be flexible in our understanding, rather than rigid and clear with only one answer. From Roman mythology we know Eros by the names of Cupid or Amor. In Hesiod's origin story, he suggests first there was Chaos, and then Eros, as the primordial connecting principle, was the one to follow and create harmony and order out of Chaos. In Plato's *Symposium*, Eros is described not as a god, but as a *daimon*, an intermediary between human and divine; which is like soul, anima, and animus. In Apuleius' version that we are examining closely in this book, Eros is a winged-*puer*—the son-lover of Aphrodite. He is the god of Love who shoots the magic arrow, but does so at Aphrodite's bidding. Thus, through the tale we can see that Love falls in love with soul; he does so through the fated prick of his own arrow when he was sent to destroy the beautiful Psyche. Is it fate or is it accidental? This is a question that remains unknowable. After Psyche reveals her husband's identity as Love himself, he flies up into a cypress tree and tells her of the fated-accident: "I, the famous archer, wounded myself with my own weapons and made you my wife" (Apuleius, 1998 trans., p. 89). Many times, we need a fated-accident to push us along on our journey—it seems this is true for Love maybe most of all. To punish Psyche for her betrayal, Eros leaves her. He knows he is reckless and irresponsible, that is why he took her as his lover disregarding his mother's wishes entirely. However, we can only surmise that this *puer* version of Eros is also grieving lost love while Psyche is suffering through Aphrodite's tasks—Eros too is broken-hearted. Here we have the familiar set up of impossible love: Eros and Psyche love each other, but cannot be together due to Aphrodite's jealous wrath—this impossibility is soul-making.

While Aphrodite sees human love as far inferior to Divine love, I am suggesting that divine love and banal love are the same—that human love is a way of expressing divine love. There are always both, the divine and the banal aspect, and that is one of the greatest paradoxes we must come to accept. Von Franz tells a story of a woman occupied with this problem who had a dream of a king and queen walking ahead of her, accompanied by a cock and a hen, who then hears a disembodied voice tell her "these two pairs are one and the same thing" (1990, p. 101). The alchemical symbol of the *coniunctio* can be represented equally as king and queen, god and goddess, or as two mating dogs. The alchemists knew that these are all aspects of the same union, symbols of the psychic opposites that comprise the personality.

Romantic love convinces us to risk everything, which leads us to ourselves; paradoxically, the more individual we become, the more we serve the greater good. As you read this book, pay attention to the ways the story works on your psyche and is present in your lived experience, in your dream life, and imaginal life. Become curious, become aware, try not to judge, just observe and see what it brings forward within you. If your romantic life is a cause of frustration for you, see if you can divert that energy into personal reflection or creative work. If a figure is regularly appearing and catching your fascination, see if you can foster a relationship with it imaginally.

What does it mean to awaken?

Around midlife we go through a spiritual awakening, maybe imagined as coming into relationship with the Self, or maybe as coming into relationship with the pantheon of archetypes that reside within us, or both; but the ego becomes aware of Something that is Greater. That Something shakes us awake and causes the ground to fall out from under our feet: maybe children, maybe a crisis, maybe the disillusionment in romantic love—which is a common one. There are numerous possibilities. At that point, we may struggle and strive to make meaning, to understand, to receive guidance, to control, and finally, to wake up! The ego gets jostled in facing challenge after challenge, until we become *conscious* of the *unconscious*—in other words, we awaken to the archetypal forces that are ever-acting upon and through us and we awaken to ourselves, our most authentic nature unfettered by cultural norms or ideals. After much effort we learn, ironically, to *just be ourselves*. The aim, if there is an aim, is to simply live one's life after the hard-won reward of waking up. There is so much wit and wisdom in the simplicity of "just being," yet it is necessary to go through the discomfort involved in awakening. Ultimately, we each find our own personal way of being in the world, and then, *with consciousness* and *love*, just live. The transformative journey of individuation is one of paradox and on-going reconciliation of often seemingly disparate perspectives. It is a journey of creating a uniquely ensouled, beautiful life. Engagement with the archetypal world offers a way of being in the world that reveres soul, love, and beauty. Through the lens of the soul, individuation is not only about the pursuit of consciousness but, also, the soul's compulsive yearning and desire for what she loves, which is love. It is not either *consciousness* or *love*, but both consciousness and love.

Yet it is necessary to strive, otherwise we remain zombielike, the walking dead, never really living our own life or being free of the internalized parental figures who are critical and rejecting of our personal ideas and values. It can be too easy, and too common, to say, "I'm just living my life," as an excuse to not "wake up," but in fact this is life *unconsciously* lived. Ultimately, we strive to find a new way of being in the world, and then, eventually, we respond and create from personal attunement to self and other. To apply alchemy to this stage, this is the completion of the second stage where the soul rejoins the body—after the first stage of *unio mentalis*—when we come into relationship with our own minds. In the second stage, the mind and body unite, but with consciousness intact and not in the form of a regression to the previous, unconscious condition. The psyche has been reorganized around the Self and the ego is in service to the Self, or the whole soul.

There are many ways to reject life—especially after betrayal and heartbreak. We may succumb to addictions or stay in destructive relationships or jobs, or simply follow the modern ideal of uninterrupted activity, go-go-go; never allowing the slower receptivity of the feminine to be honored—not being with our own Being. It is much harder and more terrifying to really live life. It is incredibly risky, and suffering is unavoidable if we choose to "hide in the middle of the flames" (Woodman, 1993, p. 8). When we practice joy, gratitude, and beauty we open our heart to love. In a concrete way, we can practice joy by setting a goal to experience joy at least once a day—for a moment, for an hour. Maybe we experience it in a walk in nature, a glimpse of beauty in the fields, the way the light glows through the clouds, or glistens on a rain drop. We can write it down when we are first practicing, making it an intentional process. Beauty opens us to experiencing joy; joy opens our hearts. From open-heartedness, we feel both deep calm and expansive.

Some of us have also denied embodied experience by engaging in spiritual ascetic practices; I have too, at a time after heartbreak, when my preference was to be with the spirit world rather than the human. A few years later, and well into my personal metamorphosis, I ached to really live far out on the high limb *and* deep down into the roots. Then a few more years again, and I just wanted a simple life—less digging around in the psyche and more just living my life: walking my son to school, cooking meals, having good conversation. When I reach the end of my

23

life, I want to feel that I loved, laughed, and cried with all that I had, that is where this journey has taken me thus far. It is not that I want to *do* more; in fact, I prefer to do less, but to do it from my heart. I want to be fully engaged in living. The choice to live is a necessary step in soul-making, because soul wants to live embodied through us.

One and Many

Jung used the term Self to describe the centre of the unconscious and consciousness—as the mediating archetype with an impetus towards wholeness. The notion of the Self belongs to the monotheistic fantasy; however, we can simply call it the Greater in us. As part of the individuation process, the ego reorients to being in service to the Self. The "I" of ego consciousness no longer understands itself as the central organizing principle; it comes to realize its rightful place is part of that which is Greater. The Self is akin to a monotheistic fantasy or to one central archetypal figure that is the ordering principle. Jung also introduced us to the pantheon of archetypes, which he likened to Greek and Roman mythological figures. The Self can be seen as the One and the pantheon as the Many. We can also view these as Spirit, which is analogous to the One, and Soul, which is analogous to the Many. Jung's Self is a symbol of unity in multiplicity.

From the soul's viewpoint, the psyche does not require the centres and unifying aims that we find in spiritual traditions and symbols such as the Self. It is a dynamic, polycentric totality and its center lies with whatever god or myth is constellated in that moment, or oftentimes with more than one. Archetypal psychology, developed by James Hillman, doesn't recognize wholeness or totality as the telos of psychological growth. The fantasy image of wholeness and individuation belongs to classical

Jungian psychology (Jung, von Franz, Johnson, Hollis, Neumann, etc.) and is a monotheistic myth of the Self as the unifying principle. Post-Jungians have expanded the notion to include soul-making as the development of relationships between consciousness and the unconscious pantheon of archetypal forces. In other words, there is a movement away from monotheism toward polytheism as a soul perspective.

I hold both these notions and relate to them dialectically. It may seem paradoxical to toggle in conversation between a fantasy of singular wholeness and a fantasy of conscious relatedness to a pantheon. However, as they both spring forth from the psyche—as the fantasy-maker—they are useful lenses. These are not opposites that require a resolution, but rather there is a tension to hold between them. The dialectics we are talking about are: monotheism and polytheism; Self and pantheon; One and Many; and spirit and soul. These pairs, or syzygies, are related to each other—we can use them to compare perspectives, as they are all ways of imaging the ineffable in order to make it comprehensible. We don't need to decide which one is "right." We can value all perspectives if we maintain conscious relatedness to the pairings. We want to hold these pairs in tension. There is no possibility of reconciliation; they just coexist. They don't need to be polarized; they can be imagined as equally necessary, each reflecting each other. They are complimentary pairings, or two sides of one coin, and both are present in any event or moment.

I would also add atheism, such as Buddhism, is a way of making the unknowable accessible to our human consciousness. Furthermore, agnosticism can foster curiosity about the unknown by inviting us to deepen into the "not-knowing," because we can't fully know the numinous, we can only experience glimpses of it during moments of awe.

Reflection Questions

As mentioned earlier, the Reflection Questions in each chapter are designed to prompt you to journey inward and discover more about your deeper self. I recommend journaling your responses. Perhaps you want to share them out-loud with a trusted friend or therapist to deepen your exploration.

Reflect on your beliefs about romantic love. Consider what the myth of Eros and Psyche may represent for you, at this time. For example, is it a map of the stages of romantic love; a map for psychological transformation; a map for the development of the soul in individuals; or other possibilities? Journal your thoughts.

Active Imagination: Q & A

Active imagination dialogue allows access to other perspectives and insights. It is also a way to engage with the chapter material. Hopefully it inspires your journaling reflections.

Question: I see this myth as showing that the stages of romantic love are themselves a medicine, a school, and I see the tasks as a training ground for individuation, if used consciously and intentionally. The phases are a mythic map for a labyrinthine terrain that we, as lovers, can traverse for the benefit of our souls' deepening. Do you agree?

Shelby: I agree love is a teacher and I like how you are framing the various stages of love, and Psyche's tasks, as each carrying their own medicine. We are invited to confront ourselves in the mirror of another, for better and worse, both that which we disown and that which we adore. We often forget about the parts that we adore *too* much in the other—seeing in them our own unconscious strengths and gifts, which are waiting for us to claim. It is ironic how, for many of us, it can be easier to see faults in ourselves but see strengths in our partner (at least initially) that are really our own. When looking consciously at projections, many are often more comfortable looking at the qualities they're ashamed of than owning the qualities they adore in the other.

I once had a long-standing series of "dark man dreams"—like being chased down narrow alleyways at night. Eventually, *I stopped and faced the man, just too tired to run any longer. He said, "oh, finally, we have been trying to catch up to you for a long time." Other men pulled covers off a truck and revealed stacks of gold bars that glowed until the whole alley lit up in golden light. Then others revealed stacks of sacred tobacco. They were meant for me.* I awoke. It was at a time when I was experiencing unrequited love, and the person had strengths that I had not yet realized in myself. It was easier to see them in him, rather than in myself. Being in that relationship, while concurrently studying the myth of Psyche and Eros, showed me I was in a process of *becoming* and eventually revealed that there were gifts that were still in shadow. Incidentally, I learned that my family lineage brought tobacco farming to Canada, and it is a sacred plant that I have come to love growing and tending. I feel a sense of joy and rootedness in my lineage when I tend tobacco through its seasonal cycles.

Question: I found myself drawn to the image of the pregnant Psyche and the gestational discomfort, pain, and hormonal beginnings of motherhood. It prompted questions: What are the differences between "ignorant bliss" and a sustained, living relationship with pleasure? After all, didn't Psyche experience pleasure in her ignorant relationship with Eros before she brought in the lamplight of consciousness? What is the difference between pleasure in naivete and the gestational development and labor pains of Pleasure's birth? Can we say perhaps that Psyche in her integrational journey develops into the worthy bride of Love/Eros himself, but also the rightful mother of Pleasure?

Shelby: Your questions grab hold of the imagination. Jung valued consciousness as the flowering of life, the crowning achievement, or the magnum opus, while I don't necessarily agree with that completely, becoming conscious is an essential element. *Consciousness* is the difference between ignorant bliss and living with pleasure. Such consciousness is only achieved through the toil and sufferings of the heart. How can we truly know pleasure if we haven't known its opposite? In alchemical processes, when the mind rejoins with the body, we have managed to bring in consciousness while being able to stay present to the affects, and instincts experienced in the body. The soul's trials, Psyche's trials, ultimately bring about the awareness to live an embodied life, and that is a sustainable, endurable pleasure. We aren't talking about the intoxicating rush of falling in love that burns off, but rather pleasure and joy as quite simple experiences: children's smiles, flowers, sun on skin, wind in leaves, and appreciating how the beloved quietly lights the woodstove after all the labours of removing projections. Then Eros enchants daily life.

Question: When a male's psyche develops greater femininity, the masculine personality must develop as well to be able to successfully relate to and accommodate the transformations in the feminine. Can the development of Eros as the masculine principle in the myth be viewed in these terms—as a response to Psyche's development as the feminine principle? If so, the tale then tells of the development of both opposing archetypal aspects, within one psyche. I see that development happens externally to the degree that it is, at least, the grist for the mill that activates one's complexes to resolve.

Shelby: You have managed the volley between opposing positions well and arrived at a great suggestion—that the tale includes the development of both masculine and feminine. That seems true within the individual, in and because of romantic relationship, and within culture as well. As one partner evolves so too must the other. Often the partner who is evolving requires the other to as well and this creates quite a lot of friction within the relationship. Couples may grow together or fall apart at these thresholds, if one prefers the comfortable familiarity of the status quo. This is true in the collective as well, society has evolved so that ego can no longer view circumstances as a simple this-or-that, black-and-white, delineation—there is much more nuance and paradox in these myths, particularly as the pendulum swings to greater balance in the culture. I also like including the word principle (i.e. feminine or masculine principle) to describe the greater archetypal expression, but within each there are various faces, personalities, affects, perspectives, including that of the shapeshifter and hermaphrodite.

Question: I reflect on this journey as a mature single woman, by choice, at midlife. Having gone through many years of growth and reflection, I am now called to wonder if I may need to retrieve that pure feeling of Edenic love within myself that is often found in one's first real love. That simple beauty of first love is where I feel called to return to, but inwardly, like a coming full circle after the hurts and betrayals. Is this the Pleasure that Psyche births, a return to bliss but without the ignorance of pre-consciousness prior to the strife? I find the end of the tasks, particularly relevant: what is the medicine in the cask of beauty ointment?

Shelby: The myth does seem to change relative to our different life stages and the experiences we are undergoing. We can rework and be reworked by this myth many times in a lifetime. The descent to retrieve the cask of beauty ointment/ medicine seems to hold particular fascination and Mystery. Perhaps part of the significance of the cask is the realization of phenomena and mystery that is associated with the beauty of the Goddess of the underworld. The medicine in the journey to meet Persephone holds different medicine than the sweetness of the naïve maiden falling in love for the first time, which is its own medicine or initiation. Perhaps the path does wind full-circle to the sweet pleasure of first love, but with wisdom and directed inwardly rather than extrovertedly. There is certainly beauty in that notion, especially after one has been blessed and hurt by love and loss by midlife.

Chapter 2

Relationship as the Vessel of Transformation

Let's further explore the notion of relationship as the vessel of transformation and look more deeply at a few more common depth psychology terms. More Reflection Questions to prompt your thinking and another Active Imagination Q & A will come at the end of this chapter.

I'll start with a dream related to the masculine and feminine principles of the psyche: *There are two black jaguars, also called "panthera" in my dream. We are in a large structure that contains them; it is beautiful and comfortable, but also keeps them contained and seems to be all interior space, but doesn't feel like a cage. I am with a male companion and he tries to dominate the male black jaguar, who won't be controlled and attacks the man, mangling and breaking his leg in several places. The female panthera intercepts and defends us humans as an ally. It is immediately clear the male needs the female, and therefore she truly holds the power, even though physically the male is more aggressive. With poise and grace, she retrieves my friend, swings him like a kitten onto her back, and we three exit out a door. We walk with ease down a long corridor alongside the enclosure— the barriers to the enclosure are almost imperceptible. The male black jaguar is in a regretful huff knowing he disappointed the female. I urgently call out to the vet on site, who is the caretaker of the panthera pair—telling him that my friend needs morphine for the pain and that he will need to have his leg bones reset by a surgeon. The vet can administer the morphine for the pain relief and tend to the immediate wounds of the physical trauma. We call for additional help in the meantime. The female black jaguar will eventually have to go back to the male, but for now she will wait with us until her partner settles his moodiness.*

What stood out the most was the power dynamic in this dream between the female and the male black jaguars, and also the use of the word *panthera*. It wasn't the first time I had a dream that specifically used both descriptors, "black jaguar" and "panthera," so at this point I researched the etymology. Panthera is latin: *pan* – all, and *ther* – great or wild beast. In the dream, these two great cats seemed to represent the masculine and feminine principles in their raw expressions and embodied with strength, power, grace, and poise. They are representative of an internal pair, and had the sense of being long-term companions. I had the sense this all took place in the psyche as a container with imperceptible edges within a human body. We could bring our consciousness (me and my companion) to visit them; we seemed to be another type of potential pairing not expressed as an *hieros gamos,* since we were friends and not romantically connected. The female clearly held dominion because of her authority and composure, while the male was representative of the raw aggression characteristic of the instinctual, theriomorphic masculine. They reminded me of Belle and Bête, Beauty and Beast, when I journaled about them— he couldn't remain beastly in her feminine presence. She was willing to help us humans, but the male had made it unmistakably clear that they weren't ours to control. These archetypal figures will collaborate with us, but they are not at our beckoning. Her confidence, assuredness, and compassion for our human vulnerability was an expression of her grace. It is also not lost on me, they are never called panther or black panther, as I would address them consciously, in the dreams; only black jaguar or panthera. I take this to mean they belong to the *daimonic* realm than the realm of consensual reality. *Daimones*, in short, are archetypal figures knowable through the imagination, not to be confused with the Christianized version, demons.

Key Depth Psychology Concepts
How is myth relevant?

Myth expresses an internal process that is universal. Imagination is everything; whatever we imagine, we can strive towards manifesting. *But where does imagination stem from?* It is not the conscious personality that imagines—the conscious personality receives the image. Psyche, as the world's soul, is the imaginer and wellspring of inspiration. The *Anima Mundi* speaks to our personal psyche and then (hopefully) our personal consciousness in her symbolic and metaphorical language. Myth, like a magnified dream, is one of the ways that imagination is manifest symbolically. It shows us the various patterns being enacted—as though in a theater—both collectively and personally. Myth shows us the archetypes at the core of the complexes that are warring, questing, or uniting. We may experience this as internal struggle with conflicting perspectives over a decision to make; a somatic struggle as the body wrestles with differing values, between the head and the heart for example; and literal struggle in our personal relationships, work, and lives. In order to understand the deities and myths acting out as patterns in our lives, we must use double-vision to see symbolically and metaphorically. The expression of getting "hit with the proverbial two-by-four," speaks to not paying attention to the internal warring elements so that it becomes literal. Yes, myths may be lived out literally, but if we see-through to the mythic narrative,

33

we can understand and relate to the divinities, the archetypes. We can think of myth as a magnified dream that belongs to the collective—and we *are* the collective, after all, "the collective" is the collection of individuals within it—thus, myth also affects us.

Eros and Psyche, or Tristan and Iseult, for example, can be an orienting outline for those engaged in soul-making and/or the individuation process through the struggles of romantic love. Commonly, the development of the ego is seen in the myth known as the hero's journey, which is the structure for most movies and books. I would suggest that this journey is applicable to men and women, though more focused on the development of the active principle functioning in the world. Whereas the tale of Eros and Psyche is specific to the development of the inner life of soul. Love and Soul, Eros and Psyche, can be used as a guide for the tasks that everyone must face psychologically, and can also outline the lived experience of the stages of an interpersonal relationship. Myth provides a way of metaphorically understanding the outer world, the inner world, and the greater collective—pointing to a specific process that we may be engaged in. Often just realizing there is a greater process unfolding is helpful. The psyche communicates and responds in symbolic language, therefore actively working with myth is a way of relating to soul and the pantheon of archetypes.

Individuation

Individuation is a key Jungian concept referring to the phase of psychological development that begins around midlife. C. G. Jung was a Swiss psychiatrist and is the founder of analytic psychology, which belongs in the broader field of depth psychology that takes into consideration the unconscious. The Greek word for soul is *psyche*. The Greek word for communication and knowledge is *logia*. *Psyche-logia*, psychology, in depth psychological terms is knowledge of the language and communication of the psyche gained from the exploration of what is going on in a person's psychological depths, or in the person's soul. Jung offered many definitions of individuation over his prolific career. While he often described it as fully commencing at midlife, he also viewed it as a life-long process of transformation whereby the contents of both the personal and collective unconscious are assimilated into the whole personality. From this lens, the aim of the transformational process is to become a whole individual, one who is indivisible— can no longer be divided—as paradoxical opposites become reconciled. This is not a state that is ever completed as we can never become fully conscious of the unfathomable depths of the unconscious.

Lived relationships, and all the struggles that ensue, can be the catalyst for the individuation process as the external world activates the alchemical process of transformation within. Jung researched and wrote about alchemy at length; therefore, some of that mysterious language is used though this book as well, but a comprehensive exploration of it is too broad for the scope of this work. In brief, alchemy is similar to the individuation process and they both outline various stages of transformation—even though the content, or challenges, evoked by these stages are unique for each person. Both alchemy and individuation involve becoming our most authentic self, no longer limited to the cultural or societal values, beliefs and ideals we've inherited. In Jung's perspective, the relationship of the ego to the Self changes. In other words, the old, egocentric way of life gets reorganized around, and in service to, the Self. Other Jungian's, such as James Hillman, as noted, would view it differently, suggesting that the ego comes into relationship with the autonomous images of the psyche and engages in the process of soul-making. Both perspectives work for me and I will use both notions at different times. The point is that the ego recognizes that it is in service and relationship to that which is Greater, whatever that means to each individual.

In the process of individuation—which entails, among other things, differentiation from culture—we explore what feels authentic and innate to our unique individuality. This includes areas such as sexuality, relationships, values, and paradigms, etc. As we become conscious of our cultural matrix, certain aspects of the dominant paradigm may no longer fit or may need to be reimagined. Individuation is a journey that brings us into relationship with our own spirit(s) that want to incarnate through us—it involves becoming conscious of the mystery with which we are all interconnected, the web as previously described.

Tension of the opposites and the transcendent function

Directly related to the individuation process is what Jung (1929/1969) called the tension of opposites. The tension of opposites is discovered experientially as we individuate because we inevitably come into conflict with our old attitudes; any time we experience conflict in our lives we are wise to inquire if we are encountering polarized perspectives. There is a gestation period for the ideas, attitudes, or archetypes that want to be born into consciousness; they incubate until the time is right. But their emergence brings us into conflict with our old identity, which didn't include them—and may have actively repressed them. Patience is required to tolerate the discomfort. The hope is that the psyche generates a resolution to the conflict. If two or more things are in opposition to each other, in tension, then the job of the conscious ego is to hold that tension and stay present with it. So long as we hold that tension, we are preparing the groundwork for the transcendent function to arise out of the unconscious. The transcendent function ideally resolves the tension by expanding the personality, which allows us to integrate what is emerging

36

into consciousness. The experience can be extremely intense, and the ego requires discipline to stay with the process until the third thing, the transcendent function, or the new symbol, emerges. The transcendent function arises from the union of conscious and unconscious contents.

It is called transcendent because it makes the transition from one attitude to another organically possible, one that transcends the pair of opposites. If we are patient and can endure the pressure without being reactive and falling back into the old mode or unconscious state, it has the potential to create a solution between heart and mind. The opposites aren't removed. We just gain a new attitude toward them that is large enough for their *coniunctio*—their reconciliation and union. As we initially become conscious, we feel crucified because the ego suffers immensely. Jung suggests that we cannot avoid suffering, but we can avoid what's worse, which is blind suffering. To avoid blind suffering involves intentionally offering ourselves as vessels for the incarnation of the Greater. In this way, the ego's suffering has meaning, which is to make way for the Self's emergence into consciousness.

The healing of suffering is the bringing together of what seems irreparably separate or opposite—the transcendent function. There can be a symbol that arises from the unconscious that can have a healing effect on us. It could come from a dream, a vision, or some other direct contact with the numinosum, including a synchronicity. Alternately, often it is a process of building an ongoing relationship with the image or figures expressing the tension, which feels like magic, because doing so really does change our experience of the problem. Active imagination is one of the ways we can relate to the contents of the psyche that are in conflict. Relatedness can foster a new attitude toward the problem, in fact relatedness, itself, could be the new attitude in many situations; we can even say that the attitude of relationship to the autonomous aspects of the psyche *is* the transcendent function.

Culturally, we have clear ideas about what behaviors are acceptable and which ones are not. Clarity is valued over chaos, boundaries over blurriness, monogamy over polyamory, fidelity over infidelity, certainty over uncertainty, knowable over unknowable, and so on. However, soul seems to have other ideas: the heart has its own autonomy; our rational mind influences our actions, but not our feelings. Thus, often heart and mind are the opposites in many conflicts. This is a familiar problem for Westerners. Choosing *simplicity* seems to be more about just accepting what soul is drawn to rather than resisting it, but that does not necessarily mean acting on it. In fact, holding the tension between opposites is often what is required. Breaking the tension will require us to start over, until we can hold the opposites in tension long enough for a new way to arise and/or until the problem is simply outgrown; such is work of the transcendent function. If we recognize we are in a psychological death/rebirth cycle, we must not thwart the death cycle and then become annoyed when rebirth does not follow. If we thwart the death cycle by breaking the tension—regressing to previous patterns of splitting them apart over and over again—rebirth cannot come. This can go on for years. We must embrace the symbolic death (such as the end of a relationship or job). When it comes time to let something go, we have to let it go—and then venture bravely into the unknown, where the new life is waiting.

An alternate perspective on the tension of the opposites is that rather than moving us closer to a sense of wholeness, we can say we are in the process of soul-making and becoming more varied vessels. The fantasy of the tension of the opposites is directly related to the notion of moving towards one unifying archetype of wholeness, the Self; however, if we consider the tension as actively engaging in soul-making we move out of the binary, dualistic thinking of the monotheistic fantasy. As we develop fortitude to hold multiple complex perspectives at a time, we become more pliant and resilient, without being brittle or fragile. We live with paradox rather than the either-or fantasy of monotheism. Notice what enlivens your imagination in each scenario and each moment. I find in therapy I will move between these two lenses freely depending on what sparks my imagination as I actively listen to the client.

What is patriarchy and why is it important in this process?

Another important term to unpack is patriarchy. This is a social system in which males hold the dominant power and authority in government, in dictating moral norms, and in the family, where father figures rule. The modern-day Western world originated with a patriarchal system. Both Christianity and ancient Greek culture, the systems that form the foundation of current Western culture and society, privileged males. As such, we all see the world and ourselves through a patriarchal lens, at least until we become conscious of that lens. In addition to privileging men, the patriarchal system favors values such as action, domination, science, and logic, over the subtler, mysterious, passive, slower values. Patriarchal cultures around the world exhibit this lack of balance, and even though there is backlash, the patriarchal model continues to hold dominion—and it is holding on tight as we witness the insidious tenacity of far-right conservatism. Men are also wounded by the imbalance in the culture. It's crucial to make a distinction between men as individuals and the system of abuse and privilege characteristic of patriarchal culture.

It is crucial to become conscious of the layers of cultural influence enfolded into our identity. As that happens, individuals may bravely choose to leave culturally prescribed illusions behind and reclaim what feels innate—including instincts, creative dreams, values, and living what feels true. That is very hard, in part because it means disappointing or offending people whom we love. Many women within patriarchies are socialized in a way that leads them to be overly *civilized* or overly *domesticated* from birth, and that domestication affects how they express their sexuality and engage in relationships. Men are taught to be heroic and noble, to provide and protect, and that often means denying their full emotional range. Men and women separating themselves from culture to live true to their values often wonder if they are being selfish and struggle with feeling guilty—and usually a parent, partner, or supposed friend will be more than happy to reflect that guilt and shame back to them. It is a difficult task being in society while individuating. There are difficult, painful choices to make—and it takes tremendous courage to face them. Often a helpful, supportive mentor or therapist is required.

Also, part of many patriarchal cultures is capitalism. Capitalism is a political and economic structure in which trade is controlled by profit driven business owners and corporations rather than the state. Directly tied to the economic viability of capitalism is consumerism, which relies on the ever-increasing need or desire to acquire goods or services. Consumerism requires a continuous sense of lack within the consumer that must be filled by accruing more goods or services; without the sense of lack, there is no consumer. Part of the patriarchal model inherently includes a depleted sense of self-worth—often based on feelings of lack and scarcity.

Rather than seeking out scarcity's opposite, abundance—which further enforces self-valuing through consuming even more goods and services—we can focus on "enoughness." Where in your life do you experience the sense of being enough and having enough? Keep your focus there to retrain your perspective and liberate yourself from the self-devaluing mindset that capitalism requires in order for the economy to thrive. Recognizing our enoughness is subversive to the over-culture. Creating a new social order together will require balance. We want to create a balanced culture from a place of unity that embraces difference and diversity. This is the task demanded by our time, and it can only be achieved by individuating and becoming our unique, personal being.

What is an archetype?

Like many Jungian terms, 'archetype' is a difficult concept to define because an archetype in depth psychology is regarded as a living and autonomous power within the collective unconscious. We can think of it as an energetic force that is pre-existent and predetermined; it is relatively stable in character and shows up in predicable modes of behaviour, emotion, thought, and fantasy. 'Arche' signifies the first or original (*arkhe*) pattern, model, or type (*typos*). Archetypes are *a priori* instincts that structure our perceptions and experiences and govern our actions. We can regard them also as the gods and goddesses that seek to incarnate through us. In a personified form they appear as motifs or images such as mother, child, hero, and healer. I speak of them frequently as gods and goddess from the Greek and Roman pantheon such as Aphrodite, Hermes, Eros, and Chiron.

Each carry certain patterns of behaviour that we enact and affects we express, as archetypes make themselves known to us via our personal consciousness. For example, a woman may experience a bout of jealousy when her beloved admires another woman's beauty. Jealousy is a common Aphroditic experience.

41

Each archetype will have a particular perspective that is uniquely theirs and may not be compatible with other archetypal perspectives. For instance, a woman may admire a beautiful pair of designer heels; from the perspective of Aphrodite, it would be wonderful to walk in those shoes. However, from the perspective of say, Artemis, she would have no interest in heels—since they would hamper her ability to move nimbly in the forest. Or maybe there is an archetype of the accountant active in your psyche, that archetypal perspective might scoff at the cost of the heels. We can consciously engage with the pantheon of archetypes active within us through active imagination. In doing so, we can discern the various lenses through which we view a problem or situation. We can think of archetypes most simply as perspectives. I am also suggesting that monotheism and polytheism, or Jung and Hillman, or Self and soul, are also perspectives available to us. They are not concurrently compatible, but we can consider various vantage points.

Active imagination

Active imagination can be understood as a kind of visualization that isn't contrived. It is a process in Jungian psychology used to bridge the gap between consciousness and the unconscious: opening oneself to the unconscious and giving free rein to fantasy, while at the same time maintaining an active, attentive, conscious point of view. We can do this with a dream by quietly centering in a mediation and inviting the dream back through our recall. Then we allow it to dream forward as an active observer of the dream; we have to follow our curiosity and interest without passing judgement or using consciousness to direct the spontaneous flow.

Another approach is to imagine a round table where the conscious personality is chairing a meeting with perhaps 4-6 other archetypes—each offering their various vantage points on a particular issue being discussed. Maybe there is a decision to be made, and one feels pulled and confused about what to do. Sitting down with the various figures to hear them out may bring some clarity. We can also use active imagination while looking at an image and allowing ourselves to soften into a state of reverie and see if the image comes to life as an animated fantasy to observe and dialogue with; we do not want to rush or force this, it must be spontaneous. It can feel odd at first, and the critic archetype will say such things as "you made that up." That is fine, let that happen too and carry on. Later you can wonder about who is the "you" that supposedly made it up. Was it your conscious mind? Or did it emanate from some other source spontaneously? The very act of "making it up" means it was created from something within. Dismissing the creative genius who makes up such things is akin to dismissing dreams as "nothing but" left over detritus from the events of the day. If we want to have a relationship with the psyche, and the contents therein, then we must treat its images seriously and with curiosity.

Daimons

Daimons are shapeshifters that speak to us in the imaginal realms; some are allies, some are mischievous, some are guardians of our fate as assigned to us at birth, which Plato described. They are paradoxical and express themselves in both the material and immaterial realms. They defy reason. As the Western psyche is anchored in reason and logic, these mysterious contrarians shape-change into figures we no longer recognize— from fairies to infections. They become viruses, for example, that remain elusive and shape-change into new variants, reminding us of their presence. They frustrate us with their demands to be acknowledged. However, if we can remember (because our soul knows) how to see with metaphorical eyes, we can imagine what the daimons and the soul of the world might be asking of us. The healing is in the imagining.

Explorations

There are many different expressions and forms of love and relationship. For this exploration, we are specifically looking at the paradigm of romance, as it's traditionally understood in the West, as the vessel for transformation. Jung said we couldn't individuate in isolation because we required another person to activate our complexes in order to go through an individuation process. Even though we may experience strong emotion while we're quietly meditating on our own, it's when we're relating to another person that our complexes truly become activated. As uncomfortable as that affectivity is, it helps us shed the layers that no longer serve us. There are not a lot of experiences as potent as romantic love to activate those complexes and move us into the muck and sticky feelings that we don't want to feel—feelings like jealousy, shame, inferiority, and insecurity.

A mythic framework can help us understand that there is a two-fold value and role that relationships play in our lives. The first, and more obvious, is that they provide the lived experience of having a human companion to share ourselves and life with. The second, more obfuscated, is that they provide a vessel of transformation for the individuals involved—a vessel because the two individuals come together to form a third, independent thing, that is the relationship itself. That relationship becomes a container for the individuals to undergo a process of self-actualizing. It is a perilous undertaking, and like a tonic in the chemical lab, it can transform in a generative, life-supporting way, or it can become toxic and destructive—or any variant in between. Romantic love can be the vessel where alchemical operations take place, precisely because it is fraught with challenges and struggles that invite us into deeper self-reflection.

Soul loves poetry. Let's take a moment to contemplate Kahlil Gibran's (1923, page 25) reflections on Love from his work *The Prophet*. I encourage you to read the whole poem. However, I'd like focus on one section—about three-quarters of the way through—to talk about and invoke the challenges that we face through romantic love.

> But if in your fear you would seek only
> love's peace and love's pleasure,
> Then it is better for you that you cover
> your nakedness and pass out of love's
> threshing-floor,
> Into the seasonless world where you
> shall laugh, but not all of your laughter,
> and weep, but not all of your tears.
>
> Love gives naught but itself and takes
> naught but from itself.
> Love possesses not nor would it be
> possessed;
> For love is sufficient unto love.
>
> When you love you should not say,
> "God is in my heart," but rather, "I am
> in the heart of God."
> And think not you can direct the course
> of love, for love, if it finds you worthy,
> directs your course.
>
> Love has no other desire but to fulfill
> itself.

But if you love and must needs have
desires, let these be your desires:
  To melt and be like a running brook
that sings its melody to the night.
  To know the pain of too much tenderness.
  To be wounded by your own under-
standing of love;
  And to bleed willingly and joyfully.
  To wake at dawn with a winged heart
and give thanks for another day of loving;
  To rest at the noon hour and meditate
love's ecstasy;
  To return home at eventide with gratitude;
  And then to sleep with a prayer for the
beloved in your heart and a song of praise
upon your lips.

This passage captures the value of loving and the depth of its emotional spectrum: the joy, the bliss, the wonderment, the transformation, and the struggling. We must know the pains and pathologies to be able to experience the opposite. We can only understand love, pleasure, and happiness if we've also experienced the anguish of suffering, and vice versa. We can only understand the pain and sadness of bereavement or betrayal if our hearts have been opened by love. One line in particular is so profound it deserves another comment: "When you love you should not say, 'God is in my heart,' but rather, 'I am in the heart of God.'" We cannot help but view the world from the perspective of the ego, our conscious personality, and yet when we take a moment to pause and step out of ourselves we find we are an expression of divinity living through us. We are the sacred vessels that the divine expresses and experiences love through—we are in the heart of God. You can choose whichever word feels comfortable for you if "God" feels too embedded in patriarchal language.

When I started my research on the wild woman, I was at Pacifica Graduate Institute preparing to do my doctoral dissertation, which would be devoted to addressing my research question: What might it look like for a woman who is individuating and engaging with the wild woman archetype to have relationships and express her sexuality? That was my starting point. Having finished the research, and now several years later, I realized I was actually starting with the question backwards. I realized part way through the research that in fact it's the relationship, and specifically the struggles of relationship, that brings us into engagement with the wild woman archetype—in fact, with the entire archetypal sphere. It's the necessary struggles and suffering that we go through with romantic love that brings us into the realm of soul, of psyche.

Because I'm a woman and because I write experientially (or let's say, embodied), my orientation is biased towards a female's perspective; however, the experience of soul-making applies to everyone. There are different perspectives and experiences, but as it pertains to the development of the embodied soul, the process follows a pattern of integration that we see in the myth. Within the collective culture, we can quite naïvely hold a belief that men are less concerned about relationship. My experience as a clinical therapist indicates men are just as concerned as women about relationship—love and connection—and the struggles it evokes. In fact, men even seem to struggle a bit more than women because it's socially acceptable for women to express emotion around relationship struggles, while many men are still developing their emotional repertoire. Men are learning to confidently own a new version of their masculinity—a whole, emotive, generative masculinity, as opposed to a dominating and controlling masculinity. I am intentionally moving away from the currently popular expression of "toxic masculinity." I am concerned that it is on the slippery slope of becoming implicit that "men and masculinity are toxic," which is inaccurate and dangerous. Dominating, controlling, and seeking to gain power over others are abusive and therefore toxic behaviours, but I don't want to perpetuate divisiveness between men and women. We need to find our way toward having respectful regard for self and other.

Let's return to the myth. Psyche became a winged-goddess who loses her mortality and is welcomed to Olympus, which can be interpreted symbolically as a regression into an unconscious state. The human soul and ego failed to maintain their conscious relationship. This is why embodiment is so important. The wild woman/man, as an expression of psyche/soul, counteracts any regressive split between body and soul—mythically portrayed as an ascent to the realm of the gods and goddesses. By staying embodied, the human psyche doesn't lose her attachment to her humanity. The transcendent movement towards Mount Olympus and the unconscious realm of the archetypes is usurped and there is no spiritual bypass if one stays in contact with the sacred wisdom of the body. It's quite precarious, or even arrogant, to think about rewriting the ending of a myth, and I realize it's grandiose. However, since the divine is living through us, perhaps the mythic expressions of archetypal patterns can evolve—even if it is slow. By staying connected to our precious human form, we can co-create a different ending with the divinities, one where the soul is related to consciously. Imagine how beautiful it would be if we all valued and related to soul *in the world*!

We need some language to try to express what we understand as the often engendered qualities of masculinity and femininity. They can be viewed in opposition, each expressing particular qualities or traits. However, this is a dualistic perspective. Dualism is important to hold consciously so that we're open to other images such as non-binary, hermaphroditic, shamanic (shapeshifter), alchemical (*heiros gamos*), and so on. Within the dualistic pairing of masculine and feminine, alternate words that I am fond of are *sol,* solar, or yang instead of masculine; and *luna,* lunar, or yin, instead of feminine. Latin languages are embedded in patriarchal cultures; therefore, language has limitations that images or symbols do not. Find terms that are comfortable for you.

What's your current understanding of qualities of masculine and feminine? The feminine is often thought of as passive and receptive. However, there are many exceptions that expose the limitations of this view. Artemis, as an expression of the archetypal feminine, is not passive and receptive, she's the ultimate huntress and has a bow and arrow that never misses. There are historical and mythic expressions of *feminine* and *masculine,* which just don't fit in the narrow confines of patriarchal cultural norms. The collective appears to be breaking free of those constrictive definitions as more people identify with non-binary self-expression, which allows them to expand into the fullness of their being. There are other ways of talking about human qualities without dividing them between genders. One reason I like *sol* and *luna,* besides being symbols, is that they are alchemical terms, which makes them mysterious and metaphorical. How can we break out of dualistic models? Can we? Maybe we can't, because maybe we need the opposites. I'm not sure, but I am excited by the collective *kairos* as we meet emergent expressions of identity within ourselves and others.

As we consider patriarchy, let's specifically contemplate the inner patriarch—not only the out-there, disembodied culture, but the inner patriarch of each person's psyche. How has psyche been colonized? Woodman (1990) calls the inner patriarch the lecherous old father figure. She also refers to the lethargic old mother figure, who can be a worse oppressor and patriarch than the inner father. There are other aspects within us that can overthrow the previously unconscious internal father and mother figures, ones that are generative and infuse life with creativity. They are unconscious until we become conscious of them so we need to make an effort to shine light upon them within. We have to become conscious of the inner patriarchal paradigms operating within us, not just "out there" in this nebulous thing we call culture or society. "For men and women to be equal partners in the outer world, the foundations for that partnership must first be laid within themselves. As within, so without. Nothing can be achieved without, if the foundations are not firmly established within" (Woodman, 1990, p. 13). Relationships are bound to falter so long as individuals remain strangers to their inner realities. We have these two relationships going on: the external human relationship and the internal relationship. In this way, human partnership that enhances both the internal and external, is not only more harmonious, but also beneficial to society.

We are in a global community and forces of creative change have already been inspired. How we view the global village in which we now live, makes all the difference. In forging a partnership of equals between sexes, cultures, and races, we meet as respectful counterparts rather than enemies whom our inherited prejudices may have taught us to fear. For example, masculinity that is bound to an obsolete patriarchy experiences the emergence of the feminine, and thus symbolically women, as a threat.

We must release the word feminine from its bondage to gender and recognize that we all have traits that were previously stereotyped by gender. Differentiated traits, such as strength, attract strong people. We can think of the trait or behaviour, and have it be less tied to gender, in order to liberate these terms from gendered stereotypes. If we fail to do the work of bringing our own generativity into consciousness—perhaps as the archetype of the *puer* or *puella*, the slightly rebellious, eternal boy or girl—we will fall back to the old inner matriarch and patriarch that uphold the outmoded values and systems that reinforce patriarchal order. "The old petrifying mother is like a great lizard lounging in the depth of the unconscious. She wants nothing of change . . . Her consort, the rigid authoritarian father, passes the laws that maintain her inertia" (Woodman, 1990, p. 17-18). They inhibit personal growth and most importantly, as a lover of freedom, if we are unconsciously trapped in their power drives, we cannot be free nor allow the freedom of others.

The myth of the hero fighting the dragon has suffered from overkill. "In killing the dragon, we are now in danger of killing nature herself on whom we depend for life" (Woodman, 1990, p. 18). Dragon-slaying has lost the symbolic value of sacrifice that leads to transformation, and instead it has become meaningless death without rebirth. The hero's journey has itself been an expression of Patriarchal culture—the hero as the ascent and decedent of the sun god, the symbol of absolute authority. The feminine principle is symbolically likened to the lunar cycles and the dragon herself. Slaying the dragon enacts the splitting apart and separation of the feminine from the masculine, when what we desperately need is the *integration* of the unconscious feminine in order to create transformation. The dragon, akin to the alchemists' *deus absconditus* (the god hidden in matter), must not be slain but must become the living redeemer. Practically speaking, we must foster the creative impetus, and try to understand the psychodynamics of creativity.

The dream I described earlier, with the pregnant masculine figure, embodies the generative transformation that occurs when masculine and feminine principles are creatively united. In exploring and expressing creative psychodynamics one finds that soul is nourished and expands. Keats, in an 1818 letter to his brother, described it as "soul-making." Both sexes share this essential activity. The child in the womb of the man in my dream was this very book you're reading. If you recall, his water broke, and from that moment the writing of this book has felt like a gushing forth, which has often been overwhelming to keep up with. This creative process, while also self-reflective, is an act of tending soul, or soul-making. It is the masculine impregnated by the feminine—giving space within itself for the child—and doing the creative labor that brings the fruit of the *hieros gamos* into the world. This book, for me, has been the fruit of the union of masculine and feminine. Though, it is not "I" at all that writes it, I am just the caretaker of the child that wants to be birthed. I'd like to add a further amplification of that dream, but it is not available for me to fully grasp yet. In alchemy, there are 20 woodcuts of the *Rosarium Philosophorum*; the 16th woodcut is an image of the philosopher's daughter (anima-soul) returning. Something of the girl child (this book as a labour of soul love) being birthed has resonance with this woodcut. I'll let that keep simmering for the book on Alchemy.

Woodman say that soul is the essence of conscious femininity; she uses these terms interchangeably—soul and conscious femininity. We have to learn to love the body since the body is a reflection of soul. We have to learn to honour our own bodies and we have to reconnect to the primal wisdom that says we are loved and that life is our birthright. We need not prove ourselves or justify our existence. We have to connect to the knowing in our bones that life is a supreme gift that is not broken into right and wrong, light and dark, birth or death. Everything is paradox and part of the awesome mystery. With our consciousness intact, relating to the archetypes, we can refuse to identify with the devouring appetites for food, drink, sexuality, or any compulsive behaviour. Consciousness is used to help mediate the instincts.

For people that have struggled with compulsion—I think everybody has some sort of compulsion they've struggled with—it isn't as simple as just becoming conscious of the compulsion. The process is so much more mysterious and involved. We can become conscious of whatever the desire or impulse is, and even become conscious of its metaphor, its symbolic value. But we will be reminded time and time again that these compulsions and these complexes are driven from something so much bigger than we are. It takes so much work to engage with what impels us over and over again, and round and round the spiral, until we can start to shift how we interact in these situations. It requires discipline, acceptance, patience, and maybe most of all, an act of grace in order to create that transformation. By disciplining the power drives of the instincts that are damaged—because they have been abused, refused, or neglected—consciousness opens the way for love, so that we are neither devoured by our instincts nor driven by fear to battle them like a dragon to slay.

Through a conscious relationship with the psyche there is a power realignment and creative partnership that can develop; once we have the new masculine and feminine principles working internally, then we can go on to have healthy relationships in the outer world as well, not only romantic ones. Sacrifice takes the place of the meaningless murder of the dragon—a sacrifice rooted in the ego's surrender to the guidance from that which is Greater in order to transform our energy patterns. These patterns may feel comfortable, but they are destructive to the creative flow of life. Keats was ahead of his time in 1819 when he described that soul-making occured through the creative process. He was convinced that the creative process itself gave birth to the symbols of redemption which characterize world religions. "Humanity was bound together in a religion of the soul, a global religion to which the word psychology would become attached, designating, as Keats himself insisted, that a knowledge of the soul is better than worship, for in worship lay the danger of deifying human powers in a manner that arrested them in some dogmatic form" (Woodman, 1990, p. 35). With these final words from Woodman and Keats, we are reminded of depth psychology as being in service to soul, which allows us to embrace our human experience as sacred practice.

Love is the ingredient, the third thing, that ignites the imagination, it is the Eros to Psyche. This can present in any creative endeavor or connected conversation, including, but not limited to romance. In connecting with another, whether a human person or a figure of the soul, the imagination ignites. Psyche or soul requires a concrete other. This takes us back to Jung's point that we can't individuate in a cave, or on a meditation cushion in the living room. Engaging with particular people, in concrete relationships, brings the greatest transformation. Romantic, specifically strong erotic, attraction can really crank up the creative and transformative heat. Another transformative container of love and soul-making is in clinical transference. Clinicians understand that when there's a really strong transference field, for better or for worse—either a strong positive erotic transference, or a strong repulsive transference—then significant transformation can happen. The temperature goes up in the alchemical cauldron of that dynamic. The people in the temenos of relationship enter the vessel of transformation, the third thing, which is the relationship, itself. Both people remain open to being altered, including the clinician. To clarify, that does not mean boundaries are ever crossed, emotional safety is paramount. Literalizing it would have the opposite effect of therapy and care, instead it would be traumatizing and wounding.

Hillman (1983) says love is not personal; it's not about the two people. It's magical, and in fact we are vessels that love transforms through. Pathologies are the specific types of suffering that we go through with love. It has the unique ability to bring up particular types of pains. These pathologies are important because they build the necessary tension and heat things up for clarifying, crystallizing, or transforming—like heating up a ruby or an emerald in order to create the pressure that causes clarification and purification. For example, jealousy, which can be terribly uncomfortable, can show us that that love is present. Jealousy gives us important information, it tells us for example, "oh, I do have strong feelings for this person." There's something else going on and then that tension gets built up and we have to work through the jealousy. Often that means doing something really hard, and vulnerable, like having to speak up for ourselves and say, "this is hard, but, I feel really insecure about this"—while exploring and processing it. We have to feel these feelings, and do our best to articulate them and advocate for ourselves. It creates the opportunity to build security within one's self and in the attachment with the other.

Love happens to us. There's really not much we can do in order to create that feeling, that magic, that glow, that heat—any of it. It happens, or it doesn't. Irene Clairmont de Castillejo (1973) says, "Love happens. It is a miracle that happens by grace. We have no control over it. It happens. It comes, it lights our lives, and very often it departs. We can never make it happen nor make it stay" (p. 116). We can create certain conditions that indicate we're open, ready, and prepared—but there's nothing we can do to actually manifest love. It graces us, or it doesn't. Alchemist's use the word *increase* as an alternative to consciousness. The alchemists say that love will increase you. It doesn't make you bigger, better, or more conscious, but it has this effect of increase like heat rising due to the tension and being in the pressure cooker.

The pathologies and suffering then are absolutely necessary, because that is where the heat is—that is where the increase of love can occur. Without the struggles and suffering, there is no tension and then there's no transformation—because there is no heat. The feeling quality that gets aroused due to our suffering— or, in Hillman's word, the *pathologies*—are expressions of love through which we expand and increase. The increase creates the clarification, or as we could call it, the transformation. The transformation of both individuals paradoxically involves each working out much of their pathologies quite autonomously and separately—while being in relationship with each other. That doesn't mean that they're going to do their individuation work and then carry-on merrily as a happy couple. We don't know what any particular situation is going to look like, but the struggle with pathologies is going to cause some sort of significant transformation. The more struggle, the more transformation.

To bring this together with a pretty little bow—though we will talk more about it along the way—suffering can be made more endurable by finding meaning in the pathologizing or suffering. If we can find some value that makes it meaningful, then we can be with the pain much more easily. Maybe as Jung would say, it no longer remains as suffering if we outgrow the problem—or as Hillman and Keats would put it, if we make soul from the suffering. The pretty bow is: the suffering and the struggles of relationship do bring us into this transformative process that then clarifies and brings us into soulful engagement with our own individuality, with the collective, and with the *anima mundi*—that is the value. The struggles of relationship bring us to our own souls, bring us home—that's the purpose of the suffering and that's the value of these struggles with relationship. This is soul-making.

Reflection Questions

As with the previous reflections, these are for you to contemplate and perhaps journal or discuss with a friend in order to expand your own self-awareness. What is your current comfort level with language around feminine and masculine qualities? What do you consider to be the value of experiencing struggles in romance? What function do you think the imagination plays in relationships, and where do you think imagination comes from?

Active Imagination Q & A

Question: I wonder what is happening in relationships at the archetypal level. We think we do the shapeshifting, that it starts in our hearts, but what images are moving there? It's so archetypal that it makes us into living archetypes, we are inseparable from the Divine. Alchemical images, and Jung's entire opus, suggest that it is the union of the opposites that produces wholeness and healing in the psyche. But the union is inherent from the start, since there is no real separation to begin with if we consider the *unus mundus* or the innate wholeness of the psyche. Until we have achieved a sort of super-consciousness that has moved beyond the boundaries of duality (a tall order), we are likely to interpret reality and its various experiences from a limited subjective perspective. Is this why discussions about anything dualistic can be so fraught with misinterpretation because most of us are perceiving, even ideas, through our personal lenses?

Shelby: It is such an exciting time in the collective as we can see the long-standing dualistic perspectives shifting. I resonate: "It's so archetypal that it makes us into living archetypes." I can't help but think of the unification of opposites that is going on in the collective where dualism is no longer so prevalent and seemingly irreconcilable poles are reconciling and finding new expressions within the individual. I see this as a deeper realization of a cosmological reality, a *coincidentia oppositorum*—a union of opposites—at work in the world, like the *unus mundus* in alchemy. The image of a gradient or spectrum might be a beneficial alternative to the dualism based on irreconcilable opposites. Jung suggests the mandala is a symbol of wholeness and totality. These kinds of symbols can allow for a range or a both/and perspective, and acceptance of paradox. Such images help to describe these non-literal energies and experiences; however, personification also springs up naturally as a way of differentiating archetypal forces. The value of personified images in our work with archetypes is that they make archetypes more relatable to the conscious personality. We can more readily engage in an active imagination with a figure like Aphrodite, when her and all the qualities and characteristics she signifies are personified.

Question: There is the love or unity that brings two together and through which the two together give birth to a new life between them. Is the essential problem with duality less about how archetypal patterning is expressed in the blueprints of our psychic cosmos (or *unus mundus*), and more about the materialistic dualism that plagues our society's worldview? By materialistic dualism I mean thinking of soul as separate from matter, and so viewing our embodied existence as lacking something, which turns us into soulless consumers of a world we consider dead and inert, rather than alive and ensouled. Is the problem less with how we understand masculine and feminine for example, and more that we fail to see that soul is the essence of everyone and everything?

Shelby: I like how you describe the third thing that arises between the duality of masculine-feminine as love or oneness, which births new life. In that way, love becomes the transcendent function. The duality between soul and matter brings to mind an interest in the polarity of *scarcity* and *enough*. Specifically, how

58

consumerism drives capitalism, which then drives scarcity to keep the economy active and growing. Thus, having a rich, soulful interior life—experiencing our connectedness to Greater—is connected to the *unus mundus*, which is a corrective to our sense of lack, giving us the knowledge of having and being "enough." As in, our birthright of being here is enough, we do not need to prove or justify our existence.

Alchemically speaking, materialism results when the spirit is embedded in matter, and matter is associated with the symbolic feminine. "The first task that confronts us is to raise the feminine to a new level of consciousness so that matter (always associated with the feminine), instead of being experienced as dark and opaque, will be suffused with its own inner light, a radiant container strong enough to relate with vibrancy and creativity to the emerging masculine consciousness," (Woodman, 1990, pp. 14-15). We have to have discipline to bring the soul essence of the feminine into consciousness, rather than unconsciously worshipping the outworn mother in the concretized matter of things that are soulless.

Question: Is it beneficial to have dualistic and personified terms since the ultimate union of opposites first requires a clear differentiation of them? If so, how do we protect ourselves against the tendency—when we think we have a final definition of these terms—to impose those definitions on ourselves or others, and in the process colonize or repress our own soul or the soul of another? This kind of colonization of the soul evokes the geopolitical image of a conquering Western masculine consciousness that is coming to 'save' and 'civilize' the indigenous wisdom of the psyche or soul. Similarly, the ego often presumptuously invades the realm of the unconscious and the soul with its own agenda—ordering things according to its own limited and limiting ideas and standards. Usually, it ends up lost and sick in a world it doesn't understand, while it attempts to mine or exploit the resources of the soul for its own ego inflation and ego-serving aggrandizement.

Shelby: We do have to first become conscious of the unconscious contents to the degree that we can. They often appear in highly differentiated expressions that become increasingly more nuanced. The archetypes have myriad ways of presenting as we can see imaged in the gods and goddess of the pantheon, and many of them will shapeshift as well. Just when we think we have mustered some solid clarity with defining and delimiting these autonomous divinities, they will do something to undermine that conception, and shake-off the rigid framework. If the ego holds too tight to the definition it does become detrimental to the soul of self or other. Rigidity and power dynamics within the psyche, particularly with the outdated inner patriarch and matriarch, do colonize the soul and stricture the multiplicity, diversity, and ambiguity of its expressions.

This notion of the colonization of the soul is intriguing because it gives us insight into the damage that has been done externally to various cultures, and also to the *anima mundi*. Internalized colonization of the soul is manifested in being overly driven and not allowing rest—that is, rest without guilt—trying to justify our self-worth based on what we "do" in a career. Our personal value is assessed based on productivity, even at the expense of health. We use busyness as a way to not connect with the body and feel what it needs—pushing through pain, physical and emotional. In contrast, slowing down and listening to the body are essential to soul care and remembering, again, that we do not have to justify our right to existence.

Question: How is our task of holding the tension of the opposites resolved symbolically in the *coniunctio*? Does it transform the distinctive categorizations of perceived opposites into ways of understanding that are poetic, metaphoric expressions of soul rather than concrete, literal realities?

Shelby: Jung's notion of the tension of the opposites relies on the recognition that internal conflict is experienced when there are two poles of opposing perspective. Jung did place great emphasis on understanding the various polarized perspectives, masculine and feminine being one, conscious and unconscious being another. We do, however, first have to be conscious of the differentiated expressions that are in tension before we can hope for a *coniunctio,* or third thing, or symbol, to arise that allows us to outgrow the problem. It is a way of understanding the invisibles symbolically in order to express the structure of the psyche. This ongoing process is both expansive and deepening.

Psyche's First Task: Exercise

This is the first of six exercises that pertains specifically to Psyche's four tasks. I suggest you meditate and journal on these questions then ideally share your thoughts with a trusted friend who can hear and witness you; without being harmful or critical. These are in addition to the "Active Imagination Q & A," that I encourage you to also engage with. Let's recap the first task demanded of Psyche by Aphrodite in order for her to win back Eros after she shone the lamplight on him:

Psyche is to separate and sort a heap of various grains and seeds by dawn or will suffer the penalty of death. Realizing the impossibility, she weeps and decides on suicide. An army of ants comes to her rescue. They sort the seeds with great industry and accomplish the task.

Without this essential task of sorting, ordering, and organizing, there is only chaos . . . a pile of seeds. We must discern and differentiate. The ant nature is of the earth, not of the intellect—it is primal and instinctive, quiet and hardworking.

It is also chthonic, belonging to the underworld. This first task may involve the tending and sorting of the inner workings of the pair or the family. It is possible that one learns to manage and protect oneself from the dangers of the inner world or an agitated anima-Psyche; that may include moods, inflations, excesses, vulnerabilities, and what used to be called possessions. *Possessions* meaning by spiritual or archetypal powers, that grabs hold of ones feeling state. In sorting we can learn to discern and manage feelings, values, timing, and boundaries of the psyche as the sorting ground.

The seeds may include an element of potentiality. Which seed shall grow, which shall be culled? The creatures born of the earth, the ants, are instincts able to order the potentiality of the seeds of the earth. Psyche possess within her an unconscious principle which enables her to select, sift, correlate, and evaluate, and so find her way amid the confusion of the numerous possibilities. For example, when writing, sifting through the topics, paragraphs and words. So many choices to make that it can be overwhelming and paralyzing, yet somehow it magically gets organized into a book. This is the work of the ants sorting the vast number of possible seeds.

The seeds can be perceived as chaotic and an image of the collective unconscious, which represents all of the creative impulses that are not realized by a human being. They are a heap of potentialities. The seeds can't be sorted with a good mind, the intuition of the hardworking ants that are knowledgeable of the contents in the underworld is required. Learning to evaluate in this way allows us to sort out the wheat from the chaff in the unconscious. Though it looks like chaos to consciousness and can feel utterly overwhelming, the unconscious always contains paradox, therefore it also contains order. The ants represent the unconscious relation to order.

Reflection Questions for the 1st Task

What does it mean to sort? What are you sorting out in your life right now? What tiny details need your attention and require organization? What practical matters in your life (home, laundry, groceries, finances, work, creative work) require ordering and structure? What is the ant nature? What in your inner life requires sorting out at this time? What inner fires need tending and how can you tend them?

Chapter 3
The Romantic Tragedy

After my initial encounter with the lone swan that I described earlier, some time had passed with no further sightings. I had mentioned it to a few friends, and one told me it might be a swan from the nearby estuary that she had read about in our local newspaper. She knew it had been living alone for a few years. On a sunny morning in late January after our only snowfall of the season, I strolled behind my home along the slough. I heard a clacking in the trees that startled me. It was not large enough to be a bear or bobcat, so I paused to look for the source of the sound and discovered a pileated woodpecker. As I observed it, a thought occurred to me that it might be sounding an alarm. I searched across the water and spotted a white mound of what I thought was snow, until it stretched upwards its long elegant neck. The swan! It was back and appeared to be finding a spot to create a nest in hopeful anticipation of finding a mate. I watched it a long while; the spot it had selected was nestled in the bulrushes and wetland grasses. It seemed to me a suitable enough spot. I wished for it to find a mate, perhaps this would be its year.

Courtly Love

Our current Western model of romantic love is a construct that evolved out of the 11th century era of knights and troubadours. It is a little unromantic to consider modern relationships as a social construct—straight-up disappointing in fact—and yet the image of this great force that we take as its eternal expression actually had a beginning. But acknowledging that our model of romantic love arose out of a patriarchal structure during the medieval ages, doesn't discount the fact that almost nothing is so powerful as romantic love to affect the conscious personality. Only that intoxicating rush of romantic love can bedazzle the conscious personality into complete surrender. It is for this reason that love is the great transformer. The struggles of love bring us into the muck we just as soon not look at, while the elixir of love can heal the deepest wounds—which were likely also inflicted by love itself.

In medieval courtly love, the chivalrous lover accepts the independence of his beloved, his mistress, and tries to make himself worthy of her by acting bravely and honorably—and by doing whatever deeds she might desire, subjecting himself to a series of ordeals to prove to her his ardor and commitment. Sexual satisfaction may not have been a goal or even end result, but the love was based on sexual attraction. The troubadour's model of the ideal lady was the wife of his employer or lord, a lady of higher status, usually the rich and powerful female head of the castle. Courtly love was also a way for nobles to express the love not found in their often-arranged marriage. "Lovers" in the context of courtly love didn't refer to sex, but rather to the act of devotion. These lovers had short trysts in secret, which escalated emotionally, but not necessarily physically. Some historical views of courtly love suggest it was a reaction to the puritanical views of the Catholic Church. However, the Cathars were active at the time and also regarded "purity" as a rejection of the pleasures of the flesh. A point of ongoing controversy about courtly love is to what extent it was sexual. All courtly love was erotic to some degree, and not purely platonic—the troubadours speak of the physical beauty of their ladies and the feelings and desires the ladies arouse in them. However, it was unclear what a poet should do: live a life of perpetual desire channeling his energies to higher ends, or physically consummate it.

A significant tale from this era that formed our notion of romantic love is that of Tristan and Iseult. While there are many variants of the tale, I'll share the general structure of it.

Explorations

We are going to bring some consciousness to the different paradigms and structures of romantic love and relationship, and do so by mining this particular myth for meaning.

Same-sex and the myriad forms of non-binary relationships provide a paradigm in which the gender distinctions of masculine and feminine are not opposites that needs to be reconciled. Instead there are other opposites to consider, if we embrace the fantasy of the Self as the monomyth. There are other opposites to reconcile such as young and old, introverted and extroverted, thinking and feeling, sensing and intuition. Some of these refer to Jung's notion of psychological types—that we all have some psychological functions that are more dominant and developed and others that are more unconscious and underdeveloped, and will often be attracted to a partner that is our opposite.

Every couple has their own creation story that usually starts with the stage of bliss, of falling in love, and the belief that the togetherness was going to be perfect and complete. These stages of romantic love seem characteristic in the West. But then the differences start surfacing after the blissful stage of falling in love when the couple is required to get to know each other and themselves. We have to let the tensions build and differentiate from each other, particularly in seeing the opposites in terms of Jung's psychological types or functions.

When somebody notices the difference in their partner, they have to come into a new appreciation of the other's way of being in the world and take back their projections. When one partner is extroverted—requiring togetherness and people to be energized—and the other partner is introverted and not interested in social gatherings, then the pair have to figure out how to accept and support each other in their differences. Then we are free to simply see our extroversion or introversion; our youthfulness or older wisdom, as part of us as individuals rather than something inherently linked to our identity. From this perspective, there are many traits or characteristics that are simply human, rather than gendered in particular ways. What is required is: consciousness, work, empathy, dedication and commitment. Hopefully these result in an enlargement of the personalities and the enrichment of life. I want emphasizes these words—we are moving towards *enlargement* and *enrichment*, rather than growth and transcendence. Conscious relationship breaks free of the power drive and moves to the deepening and enrichment of life.

As incarnations of the union of opposites, *all* relationships—homosexual, heterosexual or any other variant—serve to represent the Self. Relationships aren't just about the inner satisfaction of the individuals involved, but are a way to affect a transformation of consciousness. They provide the crucible that transforms. A polytheistic perspective can equally be applied as an alternative to the Self model, whereby the transformation of consciousness entails a greater capacity to honor and host the myriad of the gods and goddesses wishing to live in us and through us. The source of union and connection through love leads to a reality greater than our own ego; thus love, whatever its form, whatever its path, is always an instrument of divinity. *Love is an instrument of divinity, it is a path of transformation; it serves soul, or spirit—or the Self*

68

or God, or life, of the full pantheon of goddesses and gods . . . however you want to describe that which is Greater. Love is an instrument of divinity, and as such is a healer and transformer.

Not only romantic relationship but the image of family supports the ideal of individuation as the goal of personal development, if we consider it as the process by which we each move toward a full enactment of our unique potential. That's it at its core: that we are each moving toward our own individual expression and loving relationships are excellent containers for the process. People in non-traditional paradigms, may find during this process that they are in opposition to the customs and understandings of the collective, and they are encouraged to acquiesce to the guidance that comes from within and to find the courage to choose personal authenticity over secure conformity. Individuation is the work of a lifetime, not an finite goal. This is another way of looking at the question: *what is the purpose of life?* In this context, the individuation process is the purpose of life. It is not a single event, but rather a life path and a commitment, a journey on which we do not have a clear idea of the outcome. However, having said that, I've noticed experientially and from my practice that there are particular events that occur around midlife that seem to rapidly propel us forward on the individuation path. We might be in a particular struggle that is quite intense and the pressure is really high. The individuation process at that time is amplified. Nevertheless, it is a lifelong journey to claim our own strengths and weaknesses we thought belonged to the other person. The qualities we see in the beloved might be our own strengths or weaknesses that we need to develop; in some way, we have to come into relationship to those qualities. The opposites to be reconciled are not necessarily related to gender or the binary definition of gender as we have historically understood it. In fact, because of that cultural difference, it may be the very reason that one is compelled to individuate and live authentically.

The myth of Tristan and Iseult represents a lofty ideal of romantic love that is not attainable for many. The story of Tristan and Iseult, while it aptly illuminates one paradigm for romantic love, is not a cookie-cutter model for love as a path of individuation. Here is the tale:

> After defeating the Irish knight Morholt, Tristan travels to Ireland to bring back the fair Iseult for his uncle, King Mark of Cornwall, to marry. On the journey back to King Mark, they unwittingly ingest an intoxicating love potion, which causes the pair to fall in love. The potion's effects are said to wane after three years. Though madly in love with Tristan, Iseult marries Mark; however, she and Tristan cannot help but to seek one another, as lovers. The king's advisors repeatedly endeavour to have the pair tried for adultery, but the couple continually use trickery to preserve their façade of innocence. Tristan honours and respects King Mark as his mentor and adopted father; Iseult is grateful that Mark is kind to her; and Mark loves Tristan as his son and Iseult as a wife. But every night, each has horrible dreams about the future. Tristan's uncle, Mark, eventually learns of the affair and seeks to entrap his nephew and his bride. Also present is the endangerment of a fragile kingdom, the cessation of war between Ireland and Cornwall. Mark acquires what seems proof of their guilt and resolves to punish them: Tristan by hanging and Iseult by burning at the stake. Tristan escapes on his way to the gallows, makes a miraculous leap from a chapel, and rescues Iseult. The lovers escape into the forest of Morrois and take shelter

there until discovered by Mark, near death in their love-drunk stupor. They make peace with Mark after Tristan's agreement to return Iseult of Ireland to Mark and leave the country. Tristan then travels to Brittany, where he marries—for her name and her beauty—Iseult of the White Hands, and enjoys a peaceful life with her.

The myth of Tristan and Iseult is about 1,000-years-old, from the 12th century. As mentioned earlier, it's the era that birthed courtly love, which became the model for our contemporary view of romantic life. Johnson (1983) opens his book with this: "Romantic love is the single greatest energy system in the Western psyche. In our culture it has supplanted religion as the arena in which men and women seek meaning, transcendence, wholeness, and ecstasy" (p. xi). The power of romantic love was significant to both Freud and Jung, primarily showing up in the profundity of libido and the sexual instinct. It also became the basis for their divergent views, the eventual fallout between them, when Jung (1912) named the collective unconscious as a significant variable. At the inception of courtly love, love was considered otherworldly and so there were particular spiritual ideals around courting. As I previously noted, courtly love did not (typically) include having sex, nor did it permit marriage between the two lovers. They sensed that love's intensity was otherworldly, so devotion and adoration could not be expressed physically—or aim at a personal relationship or marriage. Over the years romantic love has evolved. We now try to bring the otherworldly, our spirituality, into our personal lives along with sex, marriage, friendship, cooking breakfast, paying the bills, emptying the dishwasher, and raising children. With modern day romantic partnerships, we seek spiritual fulfillment and domestic, pragmatic fulfillment *from one human*—it's too much to ask of another, and too much to fulfill.

What has occurred in the evolution from courtly love to modern romantic love is that we've muddled the distinction between human love and divine romance—the latter of which was initially imbued with a sense of sacred worship. In the West, we make romance the basis of our marriages and love relationships, and the cultural ideal of 'true love'. In romance there is an association with passion, fire, and excitement, whereas human love involves the lived experience of relating to another individual. Through this muddling of love and romance, women have become identified with the idealized archetypal feminine. Arguably, it is also true that men have become identified with the idealized archetypal masculine for women—perhaps in the role of chivalrous knight-errant, in shining armor. The problem with this, of course, is that we become blind to the whole person—including differences, so-called flaws, and uniqueness—when we project an archetype onto someone. Initially, particularly when we are younger and less experienced in life, we are unconsciously drawn to a partner we think will bring us wholeness, completion, or totality. I've referred to this as the "white picket fence dream;" however, once we have all the pickets painted and in place, we realize "hmm, something is wrong, this isn't wholeness at all." This begins a painful disillusionment period, usually in midlife. Due to such disillusionment, we might deepen into our own spiritual aspirations in search of effective ways of achieving a sense of wholeness and completion, or even just fulfillment.

During the unravelling of the ideal, the old unconscious belief returns to haunt the pair. Whispering that true love is something else, that it can't be within the ordinariness of marriage. Logically, maybe we know "true love" is something entirely different than romantic love, and yet when we are in this model of romantic love, we believe it is the whole truth and marriage is somehow supposed to continue to glow with Eros' passion. But this stays unconscious unless we endeavour to become conscious of the belief systems that are operating within us. The first Iseult, Blanchefleur, represents the anima principle and that her rightful place is not with the hero-ego—she is not to be with the conscious personality, because she is the mediator between the unconscious and the ego. Her rightful place is beside the internal king, or mature masculine. Alchemically speaking, the two together, the king and the queen, unite and create an internal wholeness that unifies the opposites contained within the psyche. As much as the hero-ego, would like to have the anima for itself, one cannot effectively bring her into the personalized world and relate to her as a woman. She belongs in and to the psyche.

The ego, the conscious personality, must be willing to withdraw the projection of the idealized other from the person in one's life in order to relate to the animum in their rightful place as the mediating archetype that inspires imagination, creativity, and life. If Tristan as ego can relinquish the Queen as the anima, and differentiate the inner life from the outer life, a whole new world of consciousness opens up, which is closed otherwise. If someone achieves that, then the romantic tragedy would no longer be a tragedy. It would in fact move an individual towards wholeness and totality. When this sacrifice is called for, the conscious personality gets torn between two opposites: the valuing of romantic love, passion, and excitement and the commitment to a stable, long-term human relationship. In the story, these values have become so muddled that we have created a second moral code in which all other rules don't apply when we are in the intoxicating experience of romantic love. As a case study example, when a client expresses how the lure of a new person is inspiring their imagination, I encourage them to engage with the imaginal figure. Sometimes people will initially feel guilt for even having such thoughts, but then they come to understand that there is an inner partner who sparks the imagination and belongs in that realm. That is its correct place and by no means needs to interfere with the human partnership. Usually when the imaginal partner is activated, and worked with in a supportive way, one's life becomes more inspired and creative. Noticing what is attractive about the person of the inner life is important. Maybe the figure personifies a past love, when life was lighter and freer of duties and responsibilities. Coming into imaginal discourse with this figure can activate more levity, maybe one picks up an instrument that long sat in a corner, or takes up drawing that was lost to another career. The discourse with the animum is not to be literalized with a concrete other, but internally engaged. As soul spark returns, it creates the possibility for Eros to also return to the primary partnership as the imagination reanimates with anima-soul.

If the rational mind tries to find its unconscious "other half," the feminine soul, in an actual person, it gets out of balance—thus the quest for romantic love can be a quest for one's own lost soul that is seen as an idealized projection onto the other. However, if the hero-ego can remove projections from the love interest in one's life, one will find one's own soul and return her to her rightful place as a mediator. The High Queen must live as an inner reality so the hero-ego can live with a mortal person outwardly—rightly seeing and loving that person intensely as they are.

The work of removing projections will be covered later, but in short, it involves discovering our own personal strengths, weaknesses, values, priorities, ideals, and morals. The story of Tristan and Iseult reflects the values of the collective, but we have to discover which of these values belong to each of us innately. Society places a high value on loyalty and commitment to a stable, human, loving relationship—as any film will demonstrate, it is a higher value than the commitment to passion and intensity. In addition, we also want to foster spiritual relationships with the persons of the soul. As we discover our personal values, we also learn that what is true at a specific moment in our life can change. We are as dynamic as life, so each experience and how we might choose to respond to it may not stay the same as we learn to trust ourselves in each moment and attend responsibly to our embodied and ensouled experiences. As we expand self-awareness of personal values and gain trust in our internal moral compass, we are more able to accept others: one person's right or truth does not make another person's right or truth wrong, just different. We move away from opposition and opposites, and move towards dialectic and analogy for dialogue and comparison. Our expanding self-awareness allows us to hold paradox, and become curious and appreciative of differences and diversity.

The essential ingredients for relationship are affection and commitment. Romance is a completely different energy system from love and commitment. If it is romance that we seek, it is passion and excitement that we shall have—but not commitment and not relationship. *But what if I want both?!,* I hear inside myself, and from my clients. To put the love potion on the correct level, to live it without betraying human relationships, is the most difficult task of consciousness that anyone can undertake in our modern Western world. That is where we have to confront at least two moralities in ourselves: the morality of romance and the morality of human commitment. As is true with the tension of the opposites, the ego is crucified between these moral energies that seem irreconcilable until we finally learn on what level to live each truth. The truth hidden in the morality of romance is that of the soul, the inner world, it must be lived inwardly; the truth hidden in the morality of human loyalty and commitment is to be lived outwardly on the level of our relationships with other people.

At a certain point in romantic love, once the spell is broken and the projections are in the long process of disentanglement—which can happen in different ways and at different stages over a span of many years. We have the opportunity to look at our projections, at what is really going on within us, and develop the strengths and recognize the weaknesses we've been projecting. We are also gifted with the opportunity to see the other person as he or she really is, and be seen. While in the process of removing projections, we may regularly find ourselves at a crossroads: will the individual retrieve the projected portions of their soul and integrate them back into their own life or will they continue to be lived out in a projection? This question is really unique to every couple and individual, because the way forward is going to depend on each person's valuing of growth, and if growth is even possible within that couple's paradigm. Not everybody values growth, and certainly not at the same time. When this is the case, one person ends up outgrowing the other. There's no right or wrong answer for what to do in these situations—if we stay or go, or some variation that is workable. What is important is that we wrestle with the projections and try to have a soulful life that is meaningful for us, regardless of what happens in the external paradigm.

Many women, particularly younger women, are accustomed to being adored as a man's anima and may resist change from that role. But there is a heavy price to pay for this, since the man who sees her as a goddess is not relating to her as a woman; he is only relating to his own projection, his own inner divinity. If he has no relationship to her as one human being to another, then there is nothing left when the projections evaporate. Most individuals want and crave authentic connection; we want to feel seen, really seen, for who we are, flaws and all. *And*, we have to become incredibly vulnerable to allow ourselves to be seen, so we need emotional and psychological safety in our human relationships. Most people can feel the difference between truly being seen and being projected upon—even though projection is intrinsic to falling in love and an inseparable part of romance in the early days.

We have to give up the demand that the other person bear our unconscious, so that we can integrate that ourselves. Over time, we become conscious of the unconscious traits we are projecting. We have to see the person for who they are, and we have to see the anima or animus for the divine figures they are, and integrate them into our own individuality. The images or symbols of the king and queen can personify—and provide us a way to relate to—the animus and anima as psychological realities, and then we can have the human love experience in the lived world. If we can understand there are two separate functions going on, then we can free the people we're in relationship with from our unconscious ideals about what they should or shouldn't be doing or being. The surprise is that we discover that human love is also divine in its own way, and we are blessed to relate to that aspect as well.

The crucial thing to take away from this discussion is that there are two processes going on: one internal and symbolic, and the other pragmatic—pertaining to human relatedness.

Eros and Pathos

It is important that we lean into the *pathos* (the Greek word for suffering) of love and let it break us open. Love causes transmutation as we explore and investigate its various layers. This is especially important after heartbreak, when we build up protective armour and are no longer naïve and innocent about the potential hurt that can come from opening up to love. Heartbreak is not limited to romantic love, but can be a part of any expression of love—such as grief and loss of a loved one; mistreatment from a loved one or parent; divorce; disillusionment of who we hoped to become and the life we hoped to live. The possibilities for heartbreak are limitless and we are going to experience it as humans. There are innumerable types of suffering, I want to focus our attention on the suffering in primarily romantic relationships.

The value of suffering is that it can take us into deeper engagement with the Greater, including the archetypes that are alive and active in us, and our innate sense of self, and soul. Engagement with pathos is spiritual or sacred practice. Throughout a person's life, suffering and experience of the sacred can be directly connected to the individuation process and to psychological development, which makes it more endurable. The benefit of the psychological approach I'm describing is that it provides a way to find meaning in suffering. We cannot transcend nor remove suffering, it is part of the human condition. Simply accepting that suffering occurs is important. In romantic love, it's a regular experience to have an autonomous, unintegrated complex stir and bring with it intense emotional affect. At the core of a complex will be an archetype or god/goddess. Such potent affect can force the person into expanding consciousness. Making complexes conscious is essential to the soul-making process. We can ease the experience by relating to the archetype at the core with imagination.

Our pathologies such as jealousy, envy, insecurities, fear of abandonment, or overwhelm, are the stuff we want to move towards, it is the base metal that is buried in the core of us, or the lead that when transformed reveals the gold. James Hillman (2005, page 80) calls these pathologies "the bedrock of loving," suggesting that we need to go into those afflictions of the soul, because in them we will find the loving, which is the gold. Pathologies offer us information, they show us where the love is. There is no grief if there is no love. We can repress these emotions, but they want us to acknowledge them. If we ignore them, they will operate autonomously. If we love, we open ourselves to these sufferings. To not love is to not fully live.

Possessiveness is a mostly unconscious attempt to create or hold onto security: "If you do not leave me, nothing will change, and I will feel safe and secure," says the childlike ego. However, as we mature, we come to terms with the reality that we never know what will happen in life. There is no such security in a relationship, or a job, or anything. Deep security can only come from our ability to trust ourselves to know how to respond in each moment to each situation as it arises. There is no way to know how long someone will be in our lives or to know why, when, or how that someone may leave. Trying to hold on to the person with controlling behavior will not work. It will have the reverse effect and push the other away, yet—and this is so important—we must, again and again if necessary, open ourselves to trusting and loving and being loved; otherwise, we harden, and life becomes a living death.

Possessiveness is not love, because "love claims no rights" (Castillejo, 1973, p. 127). Possessiveness, although natural, is anchored in hubristic thinking, as though we can or are entitled to control and claim another person. In letting go of the old paradigm of relationship, we also have to recognize that the experience of falling in love is fleeting and does not last, and we must grieve. When Eros alights, it is magic, and we can do our best to patiently await its return; recognizing the ebbs and flows of romantic love, we can even strive to create conditions that will invite its return, even to the same relationship. However, there is absolutely nothing we can do to hold on to it, to capture it, to make it stay and continue illuminating our lives in a golden hue. If we try to capture love by trying to capture our partner and vice versa, love will most assuredly wither. Ironically, the most loving thing we can do is allow the other to follow an individual path—and to be allowed to follow our own path. In being given our freedom and in giving freedom, we create conditions for love to deepen, or return, if it has flown off for a time. There is paradox in this of course, since we also deserve honesty, trust, safety, and secure attachment. These are tensions to hold and manage: secure attachment and freedom.

Jealousy is different from possessiveness, we may feel jealous but not be possessive. Jealousy may be a very appropriate response to the grief of losing someone to someone else; it is when we try to be possessive and controlling of another that we are acting from a place that is fruitless and harmful to love. Jealousy is a particular kind of loss, or imagined fear of loss. Although most of us would *strongly* prefer to not look into our own shadows and deal with uncomfortable feelings of jealousy, it is necessary. This is an archetypal experience that belongs both to Hera as the jealous wife and to Aphrodite, who is green-eyed about anyone who does not worship her as the most beloved. As archetypal experiences, these affects are not going away. We can only learn to ride out the intense emotions, seeing them as separate from ourselves, which allows us to not be reactive to them, but responsive—accepting this particular quality of suffering as part of the human condition. It invites us to gather the courage to go within, find what is affecting us, and speak kindly to our partner about our feelings. It takes a lot of work in a relationship to honour the other's feelings and validate them.

Jealousy is horrible when we are in it, though—feeling rejected and inadequate. Although immensely painful, it has a rightful place in love and in life and is often a great catalyst for awakening to the love that is at the core. It is a normal, though tremendously difficult, but important emotion, because it tells us that love is present, as opposed to apathy or indifference, which are perhaps the coldest emotions, void of empathy. Indifference is the negation of love. As we reach midlife, many of us are able to give and receive love, and thus jealousy might show up in ways it never did before.

To love another is to continually face the possibility of loss, which inevitably leads to the experience of jealousy; and to experience jealousy is to suffer. Suffering awakens us. Aldo Carotenuto (1989) in *Eros and Pathos: Shades of Love and Suffering* argues: "We must allow for the possibility of feeling jealous and we must permit ourselves to experience it to the hilt. And this means to make the shadow conscious. It is wrong to think that jealousy can be overcome through will power" (p. 74). Becoming conscious of the jealousy we're suffering is a way to remove the projections we've placed on another, whom we may have previously deified. Now we can begin to recognize the person as human and therefore imperfect or, better said, perfectly imperfect. We become mature enough to recognize our own pettiness and neediness. Jealousy is a way to become more related to our own vulnerable humanness, and the soul.

If we have been betrayed—experiencing the nightmare of losing a partner to someone else—we are given an opportunity, with time and through the pain, to move into our hearts and learn the art of forgiveness of both self and the other. There is only one way to learn forgiveness, and that is through trust broken by the experience of betrayal. Although suffering from betrayal in love is something most of us work hard to avoid, it is a life experience that deepens us, builds character, and can make life more meaningful. Learning to forgive teaches us to open our hearts and build inner security while remaining soft. "Neither trust nor forgiveness could be fully realized without betrayal. Betrayal is the dark side of both, giving them both meaning, making them both possible" (Hillman, 2005, p. 210). Forgiveness comes from the openhearted place that is experienced beyond ego. In that light, the question of good and evil becomes moot, because all pathologizing has the possibility of soul-making. The assessment of good and evil, and all the either-or problems of the monotheistic fantasy become irrelevant because we have made the experience meaningful. However, to realize this possibility of soul-making, love is necessary. We can recognize love as an initiation of the soul, when the creative connecting function of Eros is awakening the psyche. From the perspective of *love of soul*, perhaps we can better endure the pains of impossible, frustrated, painful love—when it leads us to soul. We can recognize that it is the love of our own soul that is awakening within and without.

Envy is also different than possessiveness and jealousy; it can show us something we want or desire. To envy what someone has, or how someone is, should ignite the questions: "What is it that I want?" "What can I do to manifest that reality?" For example, someone may be living a lifestyle that we admire and idealize and seeing this brings with it the bitter taste of envy, maybe that person appears to not work very much, or to have had less struggle in their lives, or to have a nicer house, family, car, or widget. Get curious about that. Is the envy indicating that we have unrealized potential? Can we adjust and move towards that potentiality? Are there seeds that we can tend—with the help of the chthonic ants organizing the unconscious latent possibilities—that can help manifest whatever it is that we are feeling envious about? Consider whatever it is that one is envying as a symbolic. The friend who appears to not work very much: can we look at our relationship to work and see if perhaps we need to cutback, and then take steps to creatively implement that. The friend who appears to have life pretty easy: can we consider where we might be struggling, and how we can make things easier on ourselves? Maybe what is required is surrendering to the grief or suffering we are experiencing. Is there wisdom from the unconscious that can help us in that anguish? Psyche's tale reminds us that there are unseen others there to help in our darkest hours. Sometimes, we can't access gratitude or joy or love, those frequencies that can usually so easily buoy us; at those dark times, we have to ask for help from the invisibles.

Psyche's betrayal of Eros initiates the journey of assimilating femininity. Too much solar consciousness in the realm of love and Eros is actually damaging. Consciousness can be damaging to romantic love, we can over-analyze love so much that the magic and mystery get destroyed. We want to be cautious about the kind of consciousness we are bringing into the arena of love. If we minimize romantic love by saying "it's all just projection," being flippant about it, then we negate and diminish such a magical experience. Too much light is just as blinding as none at all. "Enough" light allows love to thrive.

Embracing the meaningfulness of pathologized events, such as betrayal, opens us to various stages of consciousness that would otherwise be unavailable. Nevertheless, we cannot avoid them as if it was possible to remain in the Garden of primal trust. It is through suffering that we mature and the soul develops. Once we find meaningfulness in the betrayal, we expand and deepen ourselves, we become more-varied and complex people who are rich and robust, strong and pliant.

Reflection Questions

Do you agree that in the West we believe that romantic love is the only form of "love" on which marriage or love relationships can be based? What are your thoughts on the notion that human relationship has become muddled with what once was a divine reverence? What might it mean to sacrifice the personal demand that someone should bear one's unconscious projection? What would it mean to have an inner beloved and a human relationship?

Active Imagination Q & A

Question: To transmute the obstacles of unconscious projection into conscious stepping stones towards personal and mutual growth, one must actually reclaim those projections. Do relationships provide a mirror for us to see our projections and become conscious of the hidden or unconscious dimensions within ourselves? If so, I see that being worked out in my marriage in the way that we had traditional roles for practical reasons—she did most of the home management and I did most of the income-earning. But as we have grown, we have each learned more self-reliance in taking responsibility for things we used to expect the other person to do.

Shelby: Indeed, the work of removing projections is the work of expanding consciousness and really seeing the other at the same time. I like your example of this in lived experience with your wife whereby each of you develop self-reliance in the areas you previously had the other carry. The modern home is interesting. Often couples strive to be equitable to each other in their roles and responsibility as you describe—with one more responsible for tending the homemaking and the other the business. Of course, that makes sense practically, which is why it is so common. Yet, as you noted, it meant a part of each of you remained in shadow, undeveloped. The process of taking those parts back brings an increase in self-reliance.

Question: Whether we call it projection or not, without the experience of falling truly, madly, deeply in love in life, we miss one of life's core archetypal experiences—regardless of what it becomes or doesn't become in terms of a committed relationship. There is a divine element to it, it bestows itself upon us if we are graced. It is that divine element that seems to be the something that is real and true in romantic love. It was striking to me that homosexuality basically turns the question of gender opposites into a non-issue. Regardless of the sex of your partner, each couple (and by extension each person in the couple) may experience the same range of archetypal possibilities and opposites. Does differentiating who we are outside of these prescribed norms involve a lot of un-becoming (or undoing what has been instructed by society) as we move on the path of individuation?

Shelby: As a romantic at heart (maybe despite myself), I appreciate your sentiment about the archetypal experience of falling in love. It is such a divine experience and a blessing to have it find us, even if only once through the course of a lifetime. It is truly one of the gifts of being human. Indeed, I find that the suffering that inevitably comes with it, is so endurable when we can lean into gratitude for the privilege of falling truly, madly, deeply in love. This notion of un-becoming who we have been socialized into being, is so essential to living an authentic expression of one's life. I'm not sure that Jung's version of individuation includes the word "authentic" anywhere—however, the way I would define individuation, would mean that we are ever becoming more reflective of our innate nature versus our enculturated identity. The journey of understanding all the many ways patriarchal society influences our individual lives and psyches is the work of a lifetime, since we are so steeped in culture. But it is a journey worth taking. The prescribed norm of romantic love is one of these influences on our psyche's requiring differentiation.

Question: Is a successful relationship dependent on both people individuating? To this end, does refusing to continue projecting on our partner, force us to reckon with our shadow material, the unlived life, that our partner has previously been holding for us? I wonder how narcissistic it is that we fall in love with the divine image of ourselves seen in the other.

Shelby: The challenges relationships bring us are the most effective means of bringing to light the complexes, projections, and shadow material that we have previously rejected. As soon as one in the pair starts to individuate, the other is essentially sent an invitation to engage as well. To reject the invitation creates a great degree of strife and turns up the transformational tension. This comes after we fall in love. In our Western experience of falling in love, it seems projection of the soul or divine image within ourselves is the initial, inseparable instigator of this process. Perhaps it is even the animum that creates the conditions for a human pair to fall in love, so that ultimately those figures can be realized, eventually, as the inner king and queen. Even if we are conscious of the process and stages, it is still a real archetypal experience that calls us to greater relatedness to Self and other. I don't think it is narcissistic. We aren't only seeing ourselves in the other. We both perceive the other in some ways, as well as project on them in others. Furthermore, narcissism implies that we realize we are falling in love with our own divine image, but the archetypal experience of romantic love is mostly unconscious. We don't know that we're at least partly falling in love with ourselves in what we see in the other person.

Question: Do we find ourselves by recognizing the aspects of the other that don't fit our projections, while we simultaneously find the other by recognizing the aspects of ourselves we have projected on them? It seems to me that sacrificing illusory personal projections placed onto another leads to redemption of one's soul. The paradox is that "falling in love" provides the mirror that initiates our recognition of the soul. The greatest gift we receive by relinquishing our projections is the amount of energy that becomes available for a creative life in all its forms. If we cease projecting our soul onto another, our soul returns to us as we need it. What this means is that—rather than being lost in projections—the energy of the soul can now become our own inner flame—and the energy of the soul is a creative fire.

Shelby: Romantic love, once we find ourselves engaged with its psycho-active material, asks that we revision ourselves and the other. The perspective we held gets challenged as the conflicts, internal or within the relationship, invites us to go deeper. Through the individuation process, as a result of the tensions it generates, we outgrow old perspectives and we must create a new vision. The process is paradoxical in that we find a more authentic vision of ourselves and come to see the more authentic nature of the other as well. Once that flame is lit within, the relationship between the inner king and queen can manifest as a new vision and can create a new life, one that expresses love of life.

Psyche's Second Task: Exercise

Here we engage in experiential learning of the second of the four impossible tasks assigned to Psyche by Aphrodite. The task: *To collect wool from dangerous, fierce mountain sheep before nightfall. As Psyche is about to throw herself off the river's edge the reeds speak to her and give her advice to complete the task. She is told not to go directly to the rams and take the fleece by force. Instead she is to collect it at dusk, off the low brambles, and avoid the detection of the rams. She is only to approach these aggressive beasts indirectly.*

The rams are representative of raw, instinctual, aggression—a masculine energy and power that if taken on directly will overtake the conscious personality and go on a *ram*page of destruction.

Rams are representative of a masculine dominated culture. The rams are the negative aspect of patriarchy: dominating and aggressive. Psyche is aided by the reed that is of the earth and also connected to the water of the depths; it has a graceful, soft movement and dainty song-birds can be heard from the tops of the rushes. The reed is contrary to the ram energy. It was in the reeds where I first spotted the lone swan as well! The wisdom of the reeds, urging Psyche to be patient and indirect proves superior to the raging and killing of the out of balance patriarchal principle. The reeds represent a softer, intuitive wisdom that can tell Psyche how to see in the dark without being seen. The reeds convey divine wisdom and, to hear it from the unconscious, like the ants, we must be very quiet. The instinct of truth is a whisper within the human psyche. Reeds are found in wetlands, in a liminal space between *terra firma* and water. They exist in the transitional zone of neither earth nor water, but of both— they represent a knowing that is both/and rather than either/ or, they are paradoxical. The wisdom they share comes from the space between, where things are hazy, just as they advise Psyche to venture out during the hazy light, the medial light between night and day. Reeds are also associated with music in reed instruments like the flute. In Greek mythology, Pan kissed the reeds (while pursuing a nymph) and discovered that his breath could create sounds. While there is probably another layer that could be unpacked with the association to Pan, I'll stay with the reeds as they are present in the tale—Pan is perhaps implicit. One of my favorite summertime songs comes from the red-winged blackbird as they call back and forth to each other from the reeds. The reeds themselves, with their feathery tops, appear to dance and sway to their music. Reeds have an unassuming elegance compared to the ram's aggression that makes them just right to aid Psyche.

Psyche takes the reed's advice and thus solves the problem in a peaceful way that does not harm either the rams, or herself. It challenges the modern notion of power and even abundance. Power is not to be gained by wrenching out a handful of fleece from the back of the ram and going off in triumph, nor is it appropriate to hoard excess fleece. *Enough* fleece collected in the right way is what is required. It is a good rule to take only as much as one needs and as quietly as possible. To not take enough power is to remain dominated by the internal enculturated, colonizing voices, but to over-do it can quickly become abusive and leave behind wreckage—an over-reaction that still proves the dominance of the old ghosts of the past upholding the over-culture. Psyche's way is quiet, gentle, and does not cause harm.

Through this task, I am invited to find my writing voice, the one that is softer, metaphorical, and gentler rather than forceful, too solar, and too-much. I wonder about the fate of the "marketing" of the book, and I am hoping that process can remain soulful, rather than aggressive—contributing to a scarcity mindset. There is wisdom in this task: to go gently along the edges in dim light. I can feel that is the way this book wants to be marketed. But, what will that look like in the practical terms of helping this girlchild born of the pregnant man find her way into the world? I trust I'll be shown.

As another anecdote on ram energy and marketing, a few years ago, I was invited to contribute a chapter to an anthology on a topic I had written about in *Tracking the Wild Woman*. The topic was "feminine feminism." It is a topic I like, since at this stage in my life I feel grounded in my femininity, and I consider my views feminist in-as-much as I am an advocate for equity and diversity. I didn't always feel grounded in my femininity, that came after my personal midlife crisis, which was also my midlife awakening to that which is greater, which also meant awakening to a previously unconscious relationship to the feminine principle, or soul. To be clear, that awakening process took years, maybe a decade. It wasn't quick. Also, a note on equity and diversity, equity is helping those with lesser privilege share their perspective, experience, and wisdom with the world. As a Canadian, I feel very privileged; however, I also see that women still have to work very hard to achieve *equal* (not *equitable*) recognition to our white, male counterparts. In other words, to get to the same *equal* place as white males, women still have to bear more responsibility and it takes greater effort. Again, and I cannot say this enough, the problem *is not* our white male counterparts, it is our social, economic, and political structures that were built to favour men, and it is changed only though changing ourselves because we are those structures. Patriarchal systems and institutions are made up of individuals, thus as individuals live in personal integrity, the systems change. Individually, we each have to liberate our psyches from the oppression of the unconscious and autonomous over-culture that has colonized the psyche.

So back to my essay on feminine feminism, the editor of the anthology had a brilliant marketing idea in the spirit of collaboration and "many-hands-make-light-work," whereby each author would be contributing to disseminating awareness of the book through their networks and social channels. I'm a big fan of collaboration and this model of marketing appealed to me. However, once we began the editing process of my chapter, it became clear to me that the editor didn't really understand my view on feminine feminism and it seemed they were trying to direct the essay to a tone of anger, aggression, and blame towards men. We went back and forth and I explained my position—that I did not want to contribute towards further divisiveness in the world or hostility towards men. The end result was that I felt I couldn't do more and so I withdrew from the anthology. The editor, whom I believe was well-intended, exuded ram energy that felt out of integrity for me. To continue pushing myself to work with the editor, along with all my other responsibilities, was to enact the ram energy within. Retrospectively, I can see my approach was more like Psyche's: indirect and alongside the pasture, collecting the wool from the brambles. I am not sure if the anthology was ever published.

While I am subversive to the dominant culture, one of the lessons we learn from this task is that such work can be done quietly and through the side-door so-to-speak, alongside the pasture. Academic institutions, corporations, political and judicial structures etc. that advocate for change and support diverse perspectives are transforming from the inside out, which is going along side of the pasture to collect the wool. If we challenge these entrenched institutions head-on, we can expect to be met with a battering ram. Some people are cut out for that, but maybe it is time for a gentler, kinder way.

Reflection Questions

Where in your life do you experience this quiet energy? Where in your life can you be gentler? What task might you approach indirectly or through the side door? What is your relationship to power? How much power (wool) is enough for you to achieve your purpose? What does it mean to go at dusk versus the heat and light of day? Where might you be softer with your consciousness? How can you avoid facing the ram directly? Where does that apply to your life?

Chapter 4
The Magical Other

Some more time had passed since I saw the majestic swan stretch up its neck in the snow-tipped grasses. I was casually reading through the local news and there was a photo of a pair of mute swans and their cygnets, the headline read: "Mute Swan Missing and Presumed Dead." This was in the West Vancouver community, which is about 55 kilometers by car from my small town of Squamish, BC. The article went on to report that the partner was presumed killed by a natural predator and that the beloved pair had been inhabitants of the pond for many years. It suggested that the surviving partner would instinctively seek out a new mate. I had a fleeting hope that the one in my backyard would track down the widowed swan; 55 kilometers isn't too far, as the swan flies.

But as I read on, it sounded like the pair were probably "introduced" to the pond, which would have meant there was a permit. Notably, to get a permit, its wings would have been pinioned—surgically removing a joint in the wings, which prevents them from taking flight. Yikes! However, there was no permit found in the records, nor was the surviving missing swan located. Maybe she did manage to fly off, I mused. The park authorities hoped to capture it so that it could be safely housed in the same sanctuary where the cygnets are taken each year. If authorities could capture the surviving adult swan and take it to the sanctuary, it would choose a new mate and the pair would be adopted out, following the regulations that ensure the protection of the native habitats and species. Then a fantasy occurred to me. What if the swan I saw was the same surviving swan that they were looking for? Maybe it could have flown that distance? My imagination was captured, so I inquired with a couple of local birding people—the real kind that carry binoculars—about the swan that I had witnessed and two confirmed that they knew about our Squamish swan. It had been around for a couple of years.

All of this left me with quite a lot to ponder in terms of personal reflection, mirroring in nature, projections. I certainly wanted a happy love story where the two lone swans find mates; that part was clear. Through further research, I learned that mute swans are an invasive species in Canada. Invasive species! Sheesh, how could the symbol of love and mating for life be an invasive species? The European settlers brought this particular breed of swan over in the 1870s. Symbolically, that regrettably seems to lead right into the big shame of colonization in Canada and the settlers invading the Indigenous peoples. Colonization is invasive. But the swan tale doesn't end there.

Explorations

We're now going to explore anima and animus, projection, and transference in depth and try to define the ineffable mystery, which always resists definition. We use these terms often in the field of depth psychology and yet there's a whole evolution behind these expressions.

In Claire Douglas's essay "The Passion of the Unlived Life," she cites Jung's early view in which the animus is the logos aspect of women, and the anima is the feeling aspect of men. Jung thought of them as the contrasexual archetypes of the psyche—

in other words as expressing the opposite gender of the person in which they reside. Women have a masculine archetype within, the animus. Men have a feminine archetype within, the anima. Keep in mind, this was the initial view of the anima and animus. Douglas describes how this initial view was carried forward and developed by prominent Jungian women, like Esther Harding and Emma Jung. The concepts evolved in the 70s so that anima and animus were viewed as both partly available to consciousness as border phenomenon at the junction of the personal and collective unconscious. As such, they cannot be delimited completely. These concepts, what they are, their position within the psyche, their role, and their resistance to delimitation still apply today, though the notion and relationship to these mediating figures continues to evolve, within the individual and in the collective.

Both C. G. Jung and his wife, Emma Jung, defined animus as representing the logos, the quintessence of the masculine principle and agreed that it is important for developing consciousness through rational or intellectual activity. If the energy of the animus falls into the unconscious, it can become critical or otherwise disparaging to the conscious personality of the woman—blocking her from bringing her creative ideas into the world. This is the destructive animus. The work at that point is for the woman to withdraw projections from the human man and access her own logos potential within herself. This is done through cultivating her creativity and developing her own inner feminine, according to Emma Jung. Emma Jung recognized early on how important developing the inner feminine was to developing the animus principle. This point highlights the importance of reclaiming the feminine, so that it can liberate the masculine—these two separate parts become integrated as conscious aspects of a woman's personality. This plays out in the Eros and Psyche myth. As Psyche develops, as soul develops, and becomes liberated, Eros—as the masculine principle in this tale—also becomes liberated.

Esther Harding contributes significantly to this discussion by her description of the relational imbalance between the sexes. A woman starts as a psychologically undifferentiated anima woman living a primarily unconscious life. In this initial stage, a woman holds and embodies a man's projections rather than living her own life. One way I've experienced that in my own life was by helping my partner start his own business, rather than cultivating my own vocational and creative aspirations. I was living out his dreams, rather than my own. The animus, in women, only starts to develop as a second stage of psychological development according to Harding.

Dream figures of the destructive or negative animus might be of a repressive censor, or authoritarian general, or a sense of laziness and malaise may undermine the woman's creative life. As I was first awakening to the myriad faces of the animus in my life, I would have dreams of an authoritarian General who was cruel and ruthless. I couldn't relate to him directly as he was too intimidating. Using active imagination, I brought in other helper figures who were potent enough to stand up to the General. Eventually, that relationship transformed into a helpful masculine figure and I don't very often have dreams of a destructive masculine figure any longer. Through the nurturing of a conscious relationship to these archetypal figures, a woman will notice dream images transform into increasingly more helpful and wiser figures who then actively assist the woman. Because of this, a woman will experience a greater sense of flow or ease in her life. Active imagination, inner dialogue, journaling, daydreaming these figures and conversing with them are the easiest and most effective ways to foster a conscious relationship with them and bring them out of shadow and transform their negative presentations. Express yourself to the animus with helper figures and your feeling, love, and tears. Ask questions, state requests, listen to responses, observe actions, just as though you were relating to a friend. Developing a positive animus helps a woman clarify, and stand up for her own creative works, values, and feelings. It can help her focus, analyze, and distinguish.

Douglas (1990) quotes Irene Clairmont de Castillejo's description of the stages of animus development as "aggressive animus," then "belittling imp animus," and eventually the "helpful animus" (p. 161). We go through various stages in maturing psychologically with our evolving masculine principle. Through the integration of the animus, a woman lives more independently, and becomes more conscious. De Castillejo (1973) recognized that the soul image for women is a feminine figure, a woman, not her animus. This inclusion of the anima in a woman's psyche began the movement into post-Jungian thinking that views both anima and animus figures as innate to every human psyche. Nevertheless, Harding and de Castillejo, still viewed these figures as belonging to the contrasexual gender. In other words, even though the theory was developing and hints of what was to come were already at work, at the time of Harding and Castillejo's writing (1952 and 1955 respectively) anima and animus were still divided up—depending on a person's gender they were viewed as having one or the other, not both.

The evolution of feminism also ties in with animus development. The first wave of the feminist movement—while invaluable for women's rights and a necessary corrective to the one-sidedness of patriarchy—ran the risk of initially driving women to their animus as a compensatory behavior. Without being grounded in their femininity there is a risk of women imitating men, behaving in brutal, animus-like ways because they had no self-assurance or grounding within their own femininity.

In the video *Remembering Jung* (1977), von Franz talks about her work with C. G. Jung, and relays an anecdote about Jung in India:

> Jung was really struck when he was in Southern India, which is matriarchal in their basic structure. The women are beautiful, full of dignity going around in their saris. There, it's a bit too much on the other side. In every big family, the grandmother sits at the top of the table, and rules the whole thing. There, the women are proud of themselves, and bare themselves beautifully. And with us, you have to try to be as much as possible a man to be halfway recognized. The only thing to do is to get the animus out of the way and the rest comes by itself. Then femininity recovers by itself in a natural way.

While much of Jung's work carries a colonialist undercurrent, it also challenges the one-sidedness of the overly-patriarchal, analyzing, Western mind in his subtle reverence for other cultures. The anecdote given by von Franz is no different. Jung and von Franz were dedicated to the enormous task of bringing the feminine principle and the collective unconscious, into the consciousness of the Western psyche, and in doing so probably projected this dynamic onto other cultures. This was probably at work in the way Jung perceived feminine beauty in Southern Indian women and their ability to be anchored with pride and dignity in their femininity. Von Franz suggested that it is necessary for women to get the animus out of way so that the feminine can develop, and in this way a woman will come into her own expression of femininity. The animus is not in need of further development, but we do need to come into a relationship with it as a supportive, helpful guide. Through a conscious relationship with the inner masculine, the animus becomes supportive of the feminine and her ideas—helping to bring a woman's inspirations into the world.

To continue with our tracking of the evolution of theories on the anima and animus, James Hillman in 1973 wrote an essay published by *Spring* titled, "Phenomenology of the *Notion* of Anima." In this essay, Hillman evolves the idea by making several major points that expand and transform the initial concept that Jung posited. Hillman's view is that the anima is not the contrasexual side of man, nor is it present only within the psyche of men. These notions belong to Jung's conception that opposites had to be reconciled for unified wholeness; Hillman regarded that fantasy as obsolete in favour of polytheism. Again, Hillman's conception of the psyche is not based on Jung's notion of the opposites and a singular unifying totality in the Self, but rather on a pluralistic perspective of the archetypes. Hillman's view is that the anima reflects the soul—not specifically Eros or Aphrodite—images, or erotic transference. He separated the anima from the feeling function, and suggested that it leads towards psyche, and away from personal, human feelings. Hillman theorized that the animus and anima belongs to both men and women, and may be neither straightforwardly masculine nor feminine.

Women's psychological development takes place through the cultivation of her femininity, and neglected anima, not through animus development. Furthermore, Hillman asserts that the anima is the "true base of consciousness, not the ego" (as cited in Douglas, 1990, p. 182), and that the ego's analytical efforts to integrate the anima are misguided. To this end, he encourages regarding ego from the perspective of soul where ego then becomes a servant of soul-making. Hillman suggests relinquishing personal identification with the anima by understanding there is an archetype behind the image. As the anima acts through images, it gives a sense of personal reality, which can also be called upon therapeutically. The ego is integrated into the anima, into soul; as opposed to the heroic ego attempting to bring the anima under its domain. To do that, we recognize that the anima is a personified numen whom we join on her terms, rather than integrate into consciousness. This is the ultimate sacrifice of the ego's viewpoint. As Hillman states (1974), "Human being is being-in-soul (*esse in anima*) from the beginning. Integration is thus a shift of viewpoint from her in me to me in her" (p. 124). The anima is mediatrix of the unknown, the unconscious. She communicates through images, not words or dialogue, and as such she is the archetype of psychology and soul-making. Neither the anima or animus is specifically single or plural, both can occur as either. Though Hillman cautions against calling anything feminine an anima-figure, the anima is always paired with the animus, the divine pair—and each anima figure constellates a particular animus figure and vice versa. Many of these ideas were ground-breaking in the 70s when he shared them. Post-Jungian's have followed and built upon Hillman's reimagining of these figures.

Jung's notion of psychological types needs a brief discussion here in order to understand Hillman's noted differentiation of the anima from the feeling function. Jung's model of typology is based on 8 psychological functions, which operate in pairs of opposites: introversion/extroversion; sensing/intuition; thinking/feeling; judging/perceiving. Often, we are attracted to someone who is our opposite or close to it, for example, a woman with a dominant introverted intuition function will often be attracted to a man who is dominantly extraverted sensing. This could be because the animus is that type, and/or it could be because that is the inferior function that needs development. This was the thinking prior to Hillman's reimaging of the opposite, and it can still fit today, depending on the lens being used. Typology, commonly encountered in the Myers-Briggs Type Indicator® (MBTI®), suggests each person has a configuration that expresses their dominate way of 1) getting energy, 2) perceiving the world, and, 3) deciding what to do with the information they perceive. Prior to Hillman, the feeling function in typology was regularly associated with anima and women, whereas the thinking function was associated with logos and men. As stated, most post-Jungians now recognize that the anima and animus are archetypes in the psyche of both men and women and both belong to each individual psyche.

Picking up on Hillman's suggestion that the animus/anima may be one single archetype resonates for me, as I've had dreams about the shapeshifter archetype changing genders, which informs my personal understanding of the archetype. Indeed, the dream of the pregnant man birthing a daughter at the beginning of this book falls into that category. An additional dream I shared in *Tracking the Wild Woman Archetype* (2018) was: *I am on a vague trail in a steep forest that is on fire. I pass a figure descending who is initially a beautiful woman, then transforms into a beautiful black-skinned man in rubber boots, then a beautiful woman holding a mirror that could be turned towards her or toward me as she passed. Each figure had the same charismatic quality and a mysterious, knowing, mischievous grin.* The dream lingers with me years later and continues to evolve and remain dynamic. Notably, what stands out today, at least eight years later, is the qualities portrayed in that grin, and my mystified stupor as he/she passed.

In 1984, John Beebe suggested the anima can be a trickster figure: "The neglected side of the anima, it's mercurial trickster form . . . has seldom been mentioned in the literature on the anima, but may be an essential component that frees the anima from its restriction to contrasexual manifestations" (as cited in Douglas, page 193). The trickster, shapeshifter, and perhaps, shaman archetype liberates this mediating, image-making archetype from the constrictions of contrasexual manifestation.

Another term that has recently been used to describe this figure is the *anima/animus*. From Latin, *animum* speaks to the accusative singular form of *animus*, which offers a non-binary term for depth psychology to express the transitory nature of this archetype. Using -*um* at the end neuters the noun, making it neither masculine nor feminine. This is a work-around within the limitations of languages with gendered terms.

Transference and Projection

Two other concepts central to the dynamics of romantic love are transference and projection. I hope to deepen your understanding of transference and projection, while also differentiating them, as I explore some different viewpoints on these phenomena. A succinct description of projection is that we see ourselves in whatever we look at—whether it's nature or a person, it's reflecting back to us something specific about ourselves that is at least for the time being mostly or entirely unconscious. Transference, in contrast, is seeing certain qualities in someone that actually belong to another person you have history with. Put simply, here's how to differentiate projection from transference: projection is seeing ourselves in another, transference is seeing a past relationship in another. Transference commonly occurs in therapy: the client experiences the therapist as the parent (for example), thus they are *transferring* the parental content onto the therapist. The client psychologically brings into the therapy session not only themselves, but their parent too. *Countertransference* occurs when the therapist unconsciously reacts to the client's parental transference by feeling parental towards the client. It is the therapist's role to become conscious of that exchange and use it as valuable information to inform the therapy. Again, in projection, we perceive unconscious contents of ourselves; in transference, we transfer experiences from our past relationships onto a current one. Typically, transference and countertransference are kept contained in the clinical room. However, it can extend to any significant relationship. Anytime we are in relationship, both transference and projection are always going on.

Let's look closer at transference as a paradigm of relationship in general. It occurs whenever there is close, intimate involvement—which is soul-making—and will operate with helpful or disturbing factors. We are in transference wherever we go and it is immensely complicated involving every sort of emotion and fantasy. We experience it in our personal relationships, and we also experience it with our creative works that we are intimately involved with, such as writing. As an example of transference to the work, as Rumi said, "what you seek is seeking you." I would take that to mean, in this case, that Aphrodite is seeking to be known through me. I, however, identify with Psyche, and I am seeking Eros who has flown off. I am not seeking a partner or romance, but I am seeking creative spark, inspiration, and connection to Other through the writing. Truth be told, living with the COVID pandemic has felt like existing with a layer of ice over top of everything and life feels more like surviving than thriving—I feel Eros' absence. The only way to find Eros, is to atone with Aphrodite by going through the various tasks: sorting seeds (choosing the word or image, and editing); collecting wool (finding confidence to use my voice, which is softer and metaphorical, rather than direct); collecting a goblet of water from the river Styx (staying focused with eagle vision and using great care); and, visiting Persephone to request a container of beauty ointment (remain humble, surrender to symbolic death as only mortals can in order to know the value and beauty of life). This is the transference to the work entirely on an inner level—Psyche seeks Eros through reconciliation with Aphrodite.

Within the context of the therapy setting, which is where we most commonly understand the phenomenon of transference, the therapist's role includes holding the image of the union of love and soul, or Psyche and Eros, for the client until they can unite the pair themselves. Holding a loving space for the client appeals to soul; which is different and not necessarily congruent with reflection, which expands consciousness. Whenever transference takes place in therapy what is going on can be called soul-making. If a client comes to therapy through the suffering of soul, then the therapy concludes when the client realizes that he is there to find soul/Psyche for Eros, and love for his psyche. The suffering of the psyche is the initiator, whether that suffering is occurring due to challenging human relationships, or vocational unrest—these are two of the most common reasons people seek therapy. There may be other "symptoms" such as addiction, anxiety, and depression. There is often trauma present as well, but it usually involves a relationship of some sort.

In developing Psyche and Eros, they eventually unite, which becomes the *mysterium coniunctionis*, the mysterious union, which expresses the conjunction of paradox. Hillman (1972) says, "What is taking place is the creative Eros connecting with the awakening Psyche" (p. 101). Soul and her imagination awaken through this process that began with and journeyed through the neuroses or pathology of love. We ease our discomfort by getting support through therapy, though suffering is necessary for soul-making. Hillman (1972) says, "perhaps now we may realize that the development of the feminine, of anima into psyche and of the soul's awakening is a process in beauty" (p. 101). Wherever transference takes place, which is no longer confined to analysis or therapy, soul-making is going on; in this way psychological creativity finds adequate expressions outside of the consulting room.

Now let's have a closer look at the phenomenon of projection. Jung (1969) wrote on projection in *The Structure and Dynamics of the Psyche* (The Collected Works of C. G. Jung, Vol. 8). In it, he argues:

> We tend to assume that the world is as we see it, we naïvely suppose that people are as we imagine them to be. In this latter case, unfortunately, there is no scientific test that would prove the disparity between perception and reality. Although the possibility of gross deception is infinitely greater here than in our perception of the physical world, we still go on naïvely projecting our own psychology into our fellow human beings.

This is the fundamental problem, as it were, with projection. We tend to believe things and people are as we *imagine* them to be, rather than seeing them as they are. We are essentially always looking through our own "rose-coloured glasses," we cannot perceive without our own projection influencing the perceived. The only way we can differentiate projection from reality is using the test of disparity: "Is this person behaving in a way inconsistent with how I would expect?" Until we can test the reality, we create a series of more or less *imaginary* relationships based essentially on projections of ourselves. We see projection often in the arena of romantic love. We can say that person is an *imago* or alternatively, a *carrier* of symbols.

We are always in a state of projection; all the contents of our unconscious are constantly projected onto our surroundings, and it is only by recognizing certain inconsistencies that we are able to distinguish them from the *real* characteristics or properties of the person. If we are not aware that a particular trait is a projection, we cannot do anything else but be naïvely convinced that it really does belong to the object. For example, "But I thought you loved to get up early and ski on snow days?" is a projection statement because it reveals inconsistencies. All human relationships contain these projections; anyone who cannot see this in their personal life need only have their attention drawn to the times they've experienced intense relational conflicts. *"Cum grano salis*, we always see our own unavowed mistakes in our opponent. Excellent examples of this are to be found in all personal quarrels" (Jung, 1937/1969, para. 507). Even when we expand our self-awareness, we shall never see through our projections entirely, because the mind in its natural state is always projecting—it is the natural and given thing for unconscious contents to be projected. Now to add another layer of complexity, many people who are intuitive, empathetic, and attuned will also be perceptive, thus it becomes a fine art of discernment to know when we are *perceiving* what is actually present versus when we are *projecting* unconscious contents. The discernment comes when the presence of discordance is recognized.

Projection can be compared to what Levy-Bruhl called "mystic identity" or "*participation mystique*." Jung interpreted this to apply to what he referred to as so-called "primitive" people as a pre-conscious stage of psychological awareness. It implies a magical way of relating to the world—the world has a mystique in which the pre-conscious mind participates. Well, early New Year's Day morning I went for a walk on the frozen slough, the same slough where I had seen the lone swan. Only on this particular morning I saw a pair of grand ravens incanting in the most enchanting language. This I took to be my totem omen for the year, as the encounter carried with it a feeling of mystique. What I'm suggesting is that participation mystique, and by extension projection, can imbue everyday moments with beauty, meaning, and connection to the daimonic or Otherworldliness that comes when we see-through the literal with double-vision. The double-vision includes both our sensing eyes and soul eyes that perceive in metaphor and symbol.

We really don't know we are projecting, nor is it really a problem, unless a disturbance sets in, then these unconscious relationships let themselves be known and we have to set about the work of removing or taking back projections. If the libido or life force can use these projections as agreeable and convenient bridges to the world, they will improve life. But as soon as the libido wants to strike out on another path, and for this purpose begins running back along the previous bridges of projection, they will work as the greatest hindrances it is possible to imagine. This is when things get messy in relationships or adversarial situations, since what usually transpires is a person tries to devalue the former object as much as possible in order to detach their libido from it.

At that point couples will say the worst things about each other: "He is a narcissist," "She is crazy." Removing projections and reclaiming lost energy in the form of libido is long and painful. Jung said of this process:

> But as the previous identity is due to the projection of subjective contents, complete and final detachment can only take place when the imago that mirrored itself in the object is restored, together with its meaning, to the subject. This restoration is achieved through conscious recognition of the projected content, that is, by acknowledging the "symbolic value" of the object. (Jung, 1937/1969, para. 507)

In other words, the characteristics projected onto the beloved have to be restored to oneself. I would also add that the detachment can also occur as an act of grace freeing the libido to move elsewhere. Not everyone succeeds in creating this shift through conscious recognition of the symbolic value of the object. In fact, consciousness alone is rarely enough to restore harmony where a projection is related to a core wound—usually we require an act of grace as well. Thus, also having a soul-making perspective, along with expanding consciousness, adds meaningfulness to the struggle. Hillman said this well: "Reflection is never enough. Reflection may make consciousness, but love makes soul" (1972, p. 106).

We project contents of our inner worlds onto someone else and it can be hard to know when we are in transference or projection, and to a certain degree those two phenomena can work together, particularly if we project our inner parent onto the object of our projections. We perceive in the beloved something of a hook that reminds us of a parent, which perhaps touches an old wound or even stirs a positive memory. The hook provides the impetus for the transference of the parental imago, maybe it is because the psyche wants to make it conscious for healing to occur. Of course, transference is not always something about the parental relationship, we have to also recognize the presence of other mysterious elements such as the daimon—the primal force of nature that arises from the ground of being—or the archetypes that were present that guided the individual into *that* family, *that* relationship, or *that* therapy. Nevertheless, a good many relationships remind us of something familiar because we find in the other person traces of a parental figure. Hollis (1998) says: "All projection occurs unconsciously of course, for the moment one observes 'I have made a projection' one is already in the process of taking it back" (p. 35). Projection is neither good nor bad and we tend to talk about it in a way that sounds kind of inferior or negative. It's just a phenomenon of the psyche that helps us become aware of previously unconscious content.

I believe all relationships begin in projection; I'm not sure it can be otherwise. While I appreciate the rare stories of people fostering years of friendship before deciding to be life partners and human lovers, I don't think we can begin a romantic relationship without projection. We have more romantic stories of people saying "they just knew," and that it was "love at first sight," etc. As a romantic generally speaking, I appreciate those stories too. But, of course, I know, and often the pair—if they are at midlife— know as well, that they are in the sweetness of the falling in love stage, before Psyche brings in the lamplight of consciousness. In some ways it is even more sweet knowing that it is a phase that is not meant to last, because then it can be savoured while it is present.

This gets really interesting after midlife and we are conscious of projecting—then we want to be able to discern projection and distinguish it from perception. Those who have gone through the trials and tribulations of love at least once have developed their perceptivity and can accurately intuit what is in fact there in the other person, versus projection, which is what is unconsciously within ourselves. However, what we are perceiving in the other person is also part of projection; it becomes quite hard to separate perception from projection, because the projection will also be in the other to at least a small degree. Again, the key is discordance. If what we are perceiving is not what is actually living out in the human experience, in the actual concrete relationship, and we're struggling with it, then there is discordance and we want to consider that there's projection going on. Discord can be the clue that we are not engaging in concrete reality. This shows up in thoughts like, "why isn't he or she behaving the way I would want or expect?" They aren't because they're autonomous and not a reflection of one's self. Those thoughts indicate there is projection. It seems so obvious, but it is so common. A husband is surprised and disappointed that his wife doesn't want to camp for a week in the summer when he finally hears her that she actually does not like camping at all. A woman is surprised that her husband wants to bike with his friends after work rather than have dinner with her and the kids.

Culturally, as part of the dominant myth, we are taught that marriage is to be a life-long commitment. Of course, this view is evolving as many partnerships dissolve. We each have to assess our own values as to whether or not a long-term relationship is the value we use to determine if the relationship is a success or not. There are other values such as growth, or having a good companion. When we drink the love potion, or experience "love at first sight," or "knowing in my bones," some material has been activated psychically that can contribute to soul-making and/or exploring the unconscious—causing expansion and learning about human relationship-building. Jungians such as Hollis (1998), suggest this feeling is related to the original *participation mystique* with the primary caregivers or parents in an effort to recover a lost childhood. We can consider that as the unconscious desire to return to the innocence of "Eden," as Hollis calls it. That's at least partly true in many relationships, possibly even all; however, as we get older and more mature, we also become *conscious* of seeking Eden in the other, and may no longer believe a return to innocence is even desirable. Even still, despite being more self-aware, I don't know that we can stop that process from happening. Probably the counterbalance is taking responsibility for our own emotional and feeling life, and our own active and vocational life. In developing more balance, temperance, and maturity, we're less likely to be seeking Edenic fulfillment unconsciously in others.

In other cultures, often life partnership is a political or practical survival pairing, not based on romance. This search for the magical other is a phenomenon that belongs to the Western psyche as opposed to cultures that marry for pragmatic reasons. It is not only the parental imago or the animum that we're projecting or transferring onto the beloved, but also a transcendent Other. When this occurs, we begin to recognize there's a deeper archetypal connection that we're seeking, that is likely also driven by the same archetypal force (i.e. Aphrodite in this book).

Once we begin the process—the very long, painstaking process—of removing projections from the other, then the relationship is not driven by need but by a care for the other person. We can see the other person for who that person is. What's required is a letting go of the ego's, or the conscious personality's, attempt to grasp and control—allowing ourselves to be opened by the beauty of the experience that's presented to us from the mystery of transpersonal realm. The purpose of struggling is soul-making. Love and the work of soul are inextricably intertwined. Love and soul are always together—following soul is following love; following love is following soul, and that enlarges our journey and the relationship to the Mystery. Being engaged with the Magical Other, who is beyond the human and personal realm, creates a purposeful, meaningful life.

We can imagine that the experience of falling in love happens when the animum lines up with the qualities of the person projected on, if only for a short moment. The alignment is with one's inner image of the beloved. The individual with all their human faults can't ultimately measure up to this idealized inner expectation, so one regularly falls out of love. Hollis (1994) wrote: "The man's relationship to the beloved can never be better than his relationship to his own anima, because what is unconscious in him will be contaminating his relationship with the Other, just as the Other is projecting onto him in turn" (p. 49).

111

In Hollis' description, the anima is archetypal, but in his view the experience of it is mediated by way of the personal mother. To the extent that men are unaware that the anima is within, they search for her in other women, flee her, oppress her, ask her to be Beatrice in their underworld. People without a relationship to soul will anesthetize the pain through work, drugs, food, etc. Perhaps because of the dismissiveness of patriarchy to the archetypal feminine, it can be easy to overlook the presence of the anima in dreams, in relating with others, in art and music and sport, and in fantasies and imaginings. Because the soul is unconscious, it will be projected onto others.

A person may struggle and consider the soulless conditions of working life a daily torture. No perks, no car, no key to the executive washroom, and even no raise will assuage the daily loss of soul. A person knows deep down when they are selling their soul. Maybe health issues start to emerge, and one knows no paycheck is large enough to compensate. This tragedy illustrates how necessary it is for men and women to become aware of the realities of their inner life. The frail mortal whom we project the inner other upon, with their own moods and needs, cannot carry the burden for very long. To break the cycle of falling in and out of love, one must foster a relationship with the inner beloved of one's soul.

We can see the soul in dreams, myths, fantasies as a female human, which is typically how soul is expressed in both men and women. The soul appears as a person, but we recognize this as a way the soul presents herself to us so that we can relate to her through our imagination. When we try to make an actual woman carry the soul image for us, we make it personal, as though the human woman is our soul image. The great task of our time is to integrate the archetypal feminine principle, soul, into our culture, and it will not be easy. What does each of us bring to the table?

This work must be done in the most personal ways: take the time to pay attention to your dreams and write them down; take the time to acknowledge that there are things within you that need to be felt, said, lived, or grieved. Pay attention to these aspects in yourself as well as in the people in your life. In doing so, you pay attention to your soul, rather than ask someone else to carry it for you—this is integration and soul-making.

Erotic projection is an example of the gods or goddess being activated in one's psyche. The person or object of desire is no longer just a human being, he or she has been dehumanized by being divinized. When we see a human being through our projections rather than interact with the archetypal presence through imagination or with the person as they are, then we fail to relate accurately to either and there will be a discordance. Discernment is required to understand what is real and what is thought or imagined; and yet, confusing them happens repeatedly and we can be astonished each time. We are inclined to assume that things must happen in a certain way, we have to pause and compare these intuitions or fantasies with reality. When they do not align, we can begin the process of taking back the projection. This is complicated because on the one hand, we cannot fall in love without projection, but on the other hand, we don't develop a human relationship unless we continuously work to take back our projections. Failure to recognize projection causes people to fall in and out of love repeatedly.

It would be helpful if we had rituals for symbolically withdrawing projections such as returning a physical projectile to a person who has indicated his or her projection has fallen upon a certain man or woman. A symbolic ritual would delineate psychological from human relatedness. We seem so far removed from such meaningful rites in our modern culture of "swipe right." In the latter case, we indicate that based on a static, two-dimensional photo, and a few words, there might be enough of an anima or animus projection to ignite a text chat. It is a search for the image of the person who best aligns with our inner projection, with almost no human relatedness at all. Should a pair get past that stage to falling in love, there is no ritual acknowledgment that both know they are projecting and want to be in relationship with the other. As it is generally harmonious, even Eden-like, to carry each other's projection for a time, it is only when disappointment occurs that the painstaking work begins—the person one fell in love with is not at all whom was imagined.

However, we do not want to be dismissive of love by calling it a projection—*projection is not an inferior process.* Projection just is. It is related to *participation mystique.* It is a natural phenomenon that is our way of seeing ourselves in the world. Castillejo (1973) suggests the miracle of being in love is too overwhelming an experience ever to be dismissed as a projection. "I do not believe for one moment that a projection can in itself light up the whole world. It is the love which goes with it that lights the world" (p. 118). The archetypal experience of loving is not to be minimized as projection. In romantic love, openhearted loving can be transient or long-lasting. We can experience brief interludes where the heart is open and love flows in golden rays and we are connected to the transpersonal Other through the concretized experience of love being shared between humans. It does feel fantasy-like and ephemeral because it is. The more we are able to open our hearts to the archetypal experience of loving, then we experience it in more moments, activities, and with more people—not only someone with whom there is an erotic projection. Love pours into all of our relationships, activities, and rest. Love is the currency exchanged in writing a book, or having an interview, or a therapy session, or on a hike with a friend, or a shared moment with a pet, or a laugh with a child, or the delight with the unfurling of a poppy. This is Eros to Psyche. Show up with your heart open to each new day and see what comes back to you.

We can come to recognize the soul through loving another. The external journey is the catalyst for the internal journey, and one mirrors the other. We are all animal with instinctual knowing communicated through our bodies. As such, love is meant to be lived and experienced, both in the reality of our inner worlds and in embodied human loving and relatedness, regardless of the duration of that love—we must tend both relationships. Allowing that transformation to occur on both the personal and transpersonal levels allows for a deepening engagement with soul. Human relationship can bring us into this conscious engagement. It can be the vessel through which we learn that we are so much more than a singular ego with all of our childlike wantings, yearnings, and expectations. Running headlong into love with another who has their own soul journey in life is enough to thwart any ego's agenda. Love inspires us to be our most complete and authentic selves. Love asks for our best. As we recognize the reality and independent personality and life of the soul, we can foster human love that nourishes the soul and complements our soul journey. That takes ego strength and courage because the journey of love and soul is the journey of individuation and that path includes suffering. It is the path for those called to be the best version of themselves.

Reflection Questions

Explore the challenge of differentiating projection from perception (what is actually there). You might consider: how can you tell if there is discord from your perception versus what is actually there (would that then make it projection)? Please describe the difference between transference and projection and how projection and transference might show up in romantic love.

Active Imagination Q & A

Question: I had a mentor who was also a friend. Over the years the relationship deteriorated and ended badly so that we no longer keep in contact. I see now that there was a powerful transference field going on and probably also additional complexity with the boundaries being somewhat blurred between mentor and friend. Though in hindsight, the power-dynamic was such that this woman was a teacher and held the power in the relationship, which was why it hurt so much to part ways. Looking back, I can see the projection because there was discrepancy and disconnect between my projection of her and my actual experience of her. It also makes me reflect on Jung's parting with Freud. How much of that was transference, or perhaps his daimon at work, or maybe just straight-up competition and inferiority?

Shelby: The relationship with your friend and mentor sounds like it was a powerful growth and healing relationship for both of you for many years. The other thing that came to mind, in addition to the projections and transferences becoming clear and the relationship no longer being of benefit, was that you perhaps outgrew her. It is the role of the teacher to have the student outgrow them, just as children outgrow their parents. One of my previous teachers, who was perhaps more gracious than most, said he felt satisfaction when his students left him because he knew he had done his work with them. He anticipated that the students would outgrow him and he hoped they would. Most mentors are probably less tactful than he was and at worst can become jealous and even sabotaging of their students. I've also had a mentor tell a group of us whom she was teaching that seeing the younger, up-and-comers reminded her of her ageing and the fewer precious years she had left on our beautiful planet. There was a personal grief involved. The other part of your comment I really appreciate is this word "discrepancy." I have used the word discord. They are excellent beacons telling us when we are seeing ourselves versus seeing the other. It isn't always as clear as we might like, but it can certainly help as guide.

Question: Is the gift of insight into our perceptions that it affords us the opportunity to investigate, reality test, and even withdraw potentially a situation of transference or projection? It seems that in doing this we heal and become more whole within ourselves. Is it possible that we are perceiving beings, and also beings that endlessly project the next deeper contents of the objective soul as we engage with it within?

Shelby: Essentially the value of perception is the awareness it brings of the projection or transference that might be going on and the opportunity to see if there is discord. We can perceive something in another that is not necessarily in projection or transference. In other words, it may not belong to the one perceiving at all—as either projection or transference—it might wholly belong to the one we perceive it in. In those cases, it requires a high degree of self-awareness of one's own baseline or "stuff," which is where the reality testing comes in. The term *participation mystique* is relevant when talking about perception and projection; it is a state of pre-conscious perception where the subject doesn't differentiate from object. It is a natural function of the psyche and we are essentially always in it, even when we are conscious that we are (i.e. we are conscious that we have unconsciousness always effecting and affecting us—we are conscious of the unconscious). *Participation mystique*, is not good or bad, or something to get rid of. The problem is that we have come to view it as a lessor state, largely because we value consciousness so highly. But we can never be fully conscious of the unconscious, only that the unconscious is a significant variable. The word 'phenomenon' creates space for that mysterious function. It is an ongoing experience and we never come to the end to it, nor do I imagine we would want to. So as consciousness expands, it only becomes more aware that it is merely the tip of the iceberg. There is a whole segment beneath the tip of the iceberg (personal unconscious, let's call it), and moreover a whole ocean that the iceberg exists within (collective unconscious where the archetypes reside).

A comment on the notion of "healing." It is such a new-agey word to wrestle with, and implies that something is broken, incomplete, not enough, inadequate, or needing repair. From the perspective of soul, maybe nothing is broken, but rather is in the process of being made into soul. I don't mean to minimize anyone's pain of feeling broken by serious injury to the soul and child-self—of course, we all have wounding as vulnerable humans—but *healing* is a term to consider critically. The self-help industry relies on individuals believing they are broken. It is an industry embedded in patriarchal capitalism, therefore, we have to contemplate: what does *healing* mean? For this moment, let's say healing is a general term meaning to get relief from the discomfort that the ego is experiencing, or to integrate unconscious contents.

Question: Is the role of the animum to embody the compensatory position in relationship to the individual's conscious identity and self-expression? Recognizing the anima or animus in projection is only made possible because of the pain of the bad fit, which leads to us feeling let down or betrayed. This can be experienced as fear, since the person might feel overwhelmed or abandoned. Is this because the content coming up from the unconscious disrupts the status quo and feels scary and threatening as we are confronted by shadow material from our personal unconscious? Is the pain a doorway, and if we make meaning out of it, does it become more endurable?

Shelby: I like what you suggest in your question, that the animum take on the compensatory position in relationship to the individual's conscious identity and self-expression. While I appreciate we want these archetypes to be clearly defined and delimited, it is not their nature. Your suggestion I would say is *mostly* accurate, but perhaps too definitive. Yes, the projection of the anima or animus might be compensating for something opposite or lacking within the ego consciousness, but it wouldn't be only compensatory. Just as dreams can sometimes be compensatory, they are not all compensating for an absence of something in the conscious life. With projection and perception, we do have to see both the gold and the ick (lead) that is projected onto the other person and therefore present in us. It is just as hard to see the gold as that requires that we step into a greater level of responsibility. As you note, it is never fun to experience discord as we realize that what is playing out with the person is projection; thus, the pain does become a doorway that we can go through in search of greater meaning and soul.

Projection is unconscious contents within the psyche; they are neither scary nor not scary necessarily, but rather the content is just what it is. The ego consciousness might assign an evaluation to it as threatening or not; for example, if the ego sees the new content as a threat to the safety it has built for the personality, then we will experience it as scary. As we have an impetus to expand consciousness as well as self-protect, the ego may be able to bring the previously unconscious content into consciousness. At that point, the projection may or may not begin being integrated by the ego.

Question: The very phrasing of "what is actually there" with regard to perception is calling to me to define. What *is* actually there? Is it the light of consciousness shining forth through the aperture of the eyes? The surrounding world in its immediacy as an immanent reality or is-ness seems to suggest "what is actually there." However, our perspectives that are colored by the storylines of our personal mental conditioning, thoughts, judgements, and evaluations filter the light, and therefore, filters our perception of reality. Transference and projection involve not only my own filtered stories, but also the psyche of another who has their own internalized script, and on an intrapsychic level is affected by my filtered gaze as well.

Shelby: It is all so hard to discern—isn't the nature of reality unknowable ultimately? Yet us philosophical types are compelled to explore these big questions. I like how you describe the is-ness of what is actually there, and yet we can never really see that clearly because the lens and filter we look through is always playing its own reel or has its own hue. And that's only one half, if the object is another person with their own perception, projection, and transference, then the nuance becomes almost indiscernible—like seeing colours that are not of this realm as the invisibles communicate with each other. It leads to the question of "which reality is more real?" Is it the consensual reality of matter and consciousness, or the greater unknowable reality that is the one dreaming us into existence? As spiritual beings in material bodies, we are able to encounter the intersection of consensual reality and the unknowable reality of the divine—the *coniunctio* of the divine in matter is soul.

Projection: Exercise

For this exercise, please think of a person that you feel a strong erotic attraction to. It does not have to be your partner, it can be a person you know, the almost-stranger at the coffee shop, a celebrity perhaps—someone who sparks intrigue and fascination. Create your own table similar to the one below and fill it out. Think deeply, without over-thinking. Let the words just flow out of you, especially with the qualities you notice and the ones that attract or repel you. The lists can be long. I suggest starting with the first three columns. Once those feel complete, then pick the top 5 (or so) qualities that have the strongest affect for you and consider where that quality is in you (the fourth column). Is it in shadow? Is it repressed? Is it a strength? Is it an area of development? What can you do to foster that quality within yourself?

Qualities you Notice:	What attracts you?	What repels you?	Where is this quality in you?

Chapter 5
Aphrodite

Explorations

We are going to delve into the topics of the goddess Aphrodite and the characteristics of desire, beauty, and Jung's theory of libido. Libido as sex drive or desire is something people often want to talk about in therapy: maybe one person has more libido than the other, maybe the libido has dissipated—there can be many ways this energy comes up because often there are inconsistencies in compatibility. The bottom line is libido is dynamic, not static, so it changes. We will start with some Jungian theory to understand this energy in a more diverse sense.

Jung and Freud had disparate views on libido, which resulted in the demise of their friendship after many years. Freud is known for suggesting that libido energy is specifically sexual energy, whereas Jung disagreed and argued that libido was a generalized psychic energy that could be diverted and used for anything creative—including, but not limited to, sexuality. Both men continued to evolve their theories over the years. Jung didn't see libido as sexual energy primarily. He saw libido as simply psychic energy that could be channeled in multiple ways. Jung set out to scientifically measure libido, to quantify it, and initially suggested that could be done with our evaluating system that is innate to us. He was referring to the psychological functions of feeling/

thinking, sensing/intuiting, suggesting that those are innate methods of evaluating our environment and deciding how we are going to respond to it. He says the problem is that evaluation can only be applied subjectively via an individual's unique evaluating process. This poses the problem of subjective evaluation, which cannot measure consciousness.

To resolve this and arrive at an objective measurement of a quantity of psychic energy, he instead looked at complexes. The constellating power of the event, or the source of the original complex, corresponds to its intensity and, therefore, its energy. We can objectively measure the psychic energy of a complex that has been activated based upon its intensity. He then goes on to list various tests that can be used to calculate recognizable changes in intensity when a complex has been activated, and he adds that it is instinctual for us as animals to perceive the slightest emotional fluctuations in others via our feeling function. Think of being with a friend who has had a significant emotional disturbance, and has become "triggered" by a complex—a complex has been constellated. It isn't difficult to perceive that when we are with the person, this is what Jung was suggesting.

Through developing his theory of libido and attempting to quantify it, he enlarged the narrower concept of psychic energy to a broader one of life energy, which includes psychic energy as a specific part. Jung differentiates "life energy" from "life force," which he calls a more universal energy. To avoid using esoteric terms like god-like energy, spirituality, Tao, or Qi, he named this life energy libido. The way he defines life energy and libido, to me, sounds close to vitality or Qi as we might comprehend it with our modern western view of an eastern concept.

Libido implies the connection of the psychic and physical— or psyche and soma, mind and body. When a given quantity of libido disappears in one form, an equivalent amount of libido will show up in another form—but it might be in the unconscious. It doesn't necessarily appear within consciousness. For example, there are frequent cases when some of the libido disappears, apparently without forming a substitute. In that case, the substitute is unconscious and the person is unaware that the libido has essentially been swallowed up by the unconscious. This can occur in a variety of forms, including sexuality, intellectuality, or spirituality. We see this when a couple or individual may have previously enjoyed a fulfilling sex life, but then something changes and the energy seems to have disappeared. This causes all sorts of challenges in the relationship, because it is so vulnerable for people—a host of insecurities are likely to follow such a change. But that libido may have gone from sexuality into the unconscious where a new life or idea is gestating; it may have gone into intellectual studies and work; it may have gone to spiritual or creative pursuits. It may have nothing at all to do with the relationship to each other, but rather, one person has necessarily redirected the energy. I found after completing the first full draft of this manuscript, I was out of energy for it. Eros had flown off or the libido had left. After a six-month break, I was reinvigorated to begin the revision process. The libido was regenerating in the unconscious during the break.

Jung (1937/1969) identifies the most important energetic phenomenon of psychic life as the "progression and regression of libido" (para. 60). Progression is the daily advance of psychological adaptation. As environmental conditions continually change, adaptation is required. The required adaptation is that of a new attitude. He's referring to psychological types once more when he says "attitude." He uses the example of a person with a *feeling* attitude who seeks to meet the demands of reality through empathy. Such a person may easily encounter a situation that can only be solved through *thinking*. If the feeling attitude reaches its

125

limits—can no longer help the individual with a particular adaptive task—the progression of libido also ceases. These symptoms indicate a damming up of libido and the stoppages are caused by the splitting up of the pairs of opposites. Here we see the theory of the "tension of the opposites"; the pairs in opposition are the thinking and feeling functions within typology. The balancing of these two opposites is required in order to regulate the process of adaption, otherwise we would become too one-sided and unreasonable. When that occurs, regression begins, which is the backward movement of libido. This is what breaks the conflict within the psyche.

Regression, or the backward movement of libido, is the most important part of the process for the unconscious. Regression allows the rejected, unconscious, inferior parts of ourselves to come to the surface, which also contain the germs for new life. This was the psychic process that was occurring during the six-months after completing this book, but it can show up in any area of life. Regression activates an unconscious content like the shadow and leads to adapting to the inner world of the psyche. Therefore, regression is a necessary phase of development; we should not confuse progression with development. Progression is not necessarily progress psychologically speaking, even though it's an essential life movement. Regression is progress in the sense that it develops materials from the unconscious. Progression is a continuous process of adaptation to our environmental, external conditions and springs from our need for survival. Regression, on the other hand, facilitates our adaptation to the inner world and springs from the need for individuation. Libido moves forwards and backwards, and inwards (regression) and outwards (progression). Progression is similar to extraversion, whereas regression is similar to introversion.

Next, Jung (1937/1969) describes what he calls the "canalization of libido" (para. 79). This is how energy is diverted—which may or may not arise from sexuality—into another activity. He uses the analogy of a river to describe canalization or diverting libido, which serves as a metaphor for the life force. That river can be dammed up and a portion of that river can be diverted into another path. With canalization, or diverting energy, only a small portion of libido can be diverted with the use of a symbol. But the symbol is necessary for transforming or diverting the libido. In order to describe the symbolic processes required to divert energy, Jung (1937/1969) refers to the rituals that various indigenous cultures have used. In one story (para. 83), he describes how the Wachandi men of Australia impregnate the land before they plant their agricultural crops. This is done through a ritual of digging a hole in the earth that is meant to be the symbol of a vagina. In doing so, they create a fertility symbol out of the hole in the earth, and put their attention there. They are meant to continue to have their fascination carried forward as their crops grow. "It is a magical act for the purpose of transferring libido to the earth" (Jung, 1939/1969, para 85). The symbol and the supporting ritual show how the libido is transferred from sexuality to agriculture, both of which are creative. Jung suggests the symbol has to emerge in an organic way— as a product of the unconscious, an intuition, or a dream—not by conscious deliberation; however, it would seem that in the ritual described above the symbol was at least somewhat intentionally evoked and conscious. Further, I find we can choose where to put our energy, and wherever we put our energy, it is likely that something will flourish and grow. For example, if we put it into studies, we are likely to learn and expand our knowledge; if we put it into a creative endeavour, we are likely to make a song, book, or content for social media; if we

127

put it to our children, they are likely to thrive; and if we put it to our relationship, it is likely to burgeon.

Jung describes a tension between instinct and spirituality. He says, "Sexuality is not merely instinctual; it is an indisputably creative power that is not only the basic cause of our individual lives, but a very serious factor in our psychic lives as well" (Jung, 1937/1969, para. 107). We could call sexuality the spokesman of the instincts. Jung says;

> From a spiritual standpoint, sex is the chief antagonist, not because sexual indulgence is in itself more immoral than excessive eating and drinking, avarice, tyranny, and other extravagances, but because the *spirit senses in sexuality a counterpart equal and indeed akin to itself* [emphasis added]. (1937/1969, para. 107)

As an instinct, sexuality is equivalent to the spirit; it is its counterpart because sexuality contains the power of procreation and thus has a claim upon the spirit. While he doesn't agree with Freud, he acknowledges the intense power that sexual energy has as an instinctual force—it can create life. It is the strongest most immediate instinct, standing out as the instinct above all other. The spiritual principle does not necessarily conflict with instinct, but only with "blind instinct, which really amounts to an unjustified preponderance of the instinctual nature over the spiritual" (Jung, 1937/1969, para. 108). In linking libido to the individuation process, Jung says, in the first half of life, our role is to gain recognition of the instinctual sphere and how the instincts are acting on us. Libidinal energy transitions from the biological to the cultural sphere in the second half of life. We find ways that we can transform that energy, typically into forms of service, and Jung suggests being in service to one's culture. Alchemically speaking, we would say the philosopher is in service to the stone at the end of the process—the individual is in service to something greater than themselves.

Aphrodite

Now let's shift our focus away from this more expanded theory of libido as psychic, life, and sexual energy, and move to a mythological perspective of Aphrodite. In addition to love, beauty, and sexuality, Aphrodite also attends to procreation and verbal creation—she impels men and women to fulfill their creativity. Aphrodite has a beautiful, golden allure, specifically for women in whom Aphrodite is a dominant tidal wave kind of force (think of Marilyn Monroe). While it's true she is often expressed in women, Aphrodite is without a doubt an archetype that's available to everyone, though probably in diluted forms due to her power. We can see Aphrodite in men who share her values too—she's not exclusive to women and she's able to be an operating mode of consciousness in absolutely everybody. We can intentionally shift our consciousness to invite her perspective in order to experience and understand her traits and characteristics.

As the goddess primarily responsible for sexual energy, she certainly has a particular perspective that she can bring to Jung's theory about libido and the power of sexual energy. We can divert sexual energy into creative endeavors, or we can express it by being a lover and in a relationship. We can also redirect that energy and it may emerge as a creative force or a creative project. For example, energy built up through an erotic attraction that is not actualized can be redirected into writing, art, building a course or a lecture, renovating a home, writing a song, or poem—the creative possibilities are endless. Perhaps there is an erotic attraction to a colleague that is inappropriate to act upon. That energy can go into a collaborative project. It could be that the psyche is longing for an unavailable man or woman, and that energy can go, not only into individuation, but also into writing a thesis and soul-making at the same time.

My experience with writing has been that it coincides with a lived romance that plays out in the external world as some type of thwarted-love. Thus, the energy builds because it is unfulfilled by the object/man of my desire. Instead, that creative impulse goes into research and writing. I wonder (with equal parts curiosity and frustration): Is this because the psyche (or, ultimately, Aphrodite) has a grand plan to provide the energy I require to give birth to a large creative project? Shinoda Bolen (1984) describes ways that Aphrodite might present in an individual's psyche: as the lover who feels attractive and vibrant; while falling in love when each is drawn toward the other's beauty that is enhanced by Aphrodite's golden light; as the procreative instinct for pregnancy; and as the creative force that comes out of intense and passionate involvement to bring something new into being. Aphrodite may act as a creative force that involves a person in a variety of affairs of the heart, and sometimes both the creative and romantic aspects of Aphrodite are present in the same person. Once one is engrossed, then an interaction between oneself and the aesthetic medium can occur and something new can emerge.

Work must be passionate and engaging for Aphrodite-women—women who have the goddess as a dominant figure in their psyche—and offer variety and intensity to keep such women interested. Repetitious tasks will be dull, such as household, clerical, or technical. An Aphrodite-woman may achieve success as a result of doing what she enjoys, but not because she sets out to do so in the same way that Artemis or Athena do. Examples of the kind of work Aphrodite-women might thrive at include: art, music, writing, dance, or drama. They may also be drawn to be a teacher, therapist, or editor, which are callings that are special to

Aphrodite. In relationships, unless other goddesses are strongly active, Aphrodite-women will gravitate towards men who are not necessarily good for them, probably choosing men similar to Aphrodite's own choice—creative, complex, moody, or emotional men like Hephaestus, Ares, and Hermes. In such cases, the task is for the woman to become aware of the pattern and look out for her own best interests, because Aphrodite certainly is not. Thus, a woman finds power in her choices and the shaping of their outcome once she has sorted out her priorities.

Shinoda Bolen (1984) suggests that Psyche's tasks are depicting the development of abilities that often feel "masculine" to women like Psyche, who need to develop them—even though they are natural attributes of Artemis and Athena. Each time Psyche masters a task, she acquires an ability she did not have before—an ability equated in Jungian terms to the animus or masculine aspect. Neumann (1956) also points out that the tasks demand the exercise of what we might typically call masculine traits. In sorting the seeds of the first task, a woman learns to stay with the confused situation and not act until clarity emerges. She has to learn to trust the intuitive process represented by the ants who operate beyond conscious control. In the second task of acquiring some of the golden fleece, a woman learns how to acquire power (rams' wool) without being destroyed by it. Athenian women can be directly involved in law, strategy, and politics, but a woman who is like Psyche does better to observe, wait, and gradually collect power indirectly. In the third task of filling the crystal goblet, women who are like Psyche and Aphrodite need some objectivity and emotional distance in order to see the overall patterns and grasp one goblet full of what is important—this prevents being overwhelmed. The fourth task is to retrieve the box of beauty ointment from Persephone, the goddess of the underworld. In this multilayered task, that is more than the traditional hero's test of courage and determination, Psyche learns to say, "No." In doing so, she learns to keep to her goal, and harden her heart to compassion. Such a woman, who has an overriding propensity to be kind, must learn to exercise her choice and not allow herself to be imposed upon and distracted from doing something of value for herself. Whether it's a person who needs company or comfort, or the allure of an erotically charged relationship, a woman can't determine her own life until she can say "no" to the particular predisposition to put others before herself. Yet, as with Psyche, her basic nature remains unchanged. She values love and relationships and will risk everything for it. One of the hardest requests for me to say "no" to is spending time with my friends. Not because I suffer from "fear-of-missing-out," but because I don't want to disappoint the people who are important to me.

I invite you to bring these two perspectives together—the mythological and Jung's scientific, empirical outlook—and see how they fit for you. Maybe they don't, maybe they do. One might resonate more easily, and one might not. The mythological approach is more comfortable for me because it speaks of symbols, which I find extremely useful. Allow this energy to work on you and observe and notice what happens internally and externally—perhaps tracking your thoughts, dreams, and lived experiences in a journal. Or, better yet, maybe there is a creative way you feel compelled to express this energy.

Beauty

One of Psyche's central and defining features is her beauty. Beauty is central to the myth and to psychological life. Psyche's beauty is different than Aphrodite's—the latter of which is a much more sexualized beauty. The beauty of Psyche refers to a sense of the beautiful in connection with our inner world. The thread of beauty is woven throughout: the tale begins because of Psyche's revered mortal beauty; Aphrodite is the goddess of love and beauty; and, one of my favorite parts of the myth, is the mystery of Persephone's beauty box. Whatever mysterious potion is in the beauty box, Persephone has it, Aphrodite wants it, and Psyche opens it—which causes her to fall into a death-like sleep. My preference is to allow this symbol of the beauty box to be ambiguous, whatever it means for each person as they read it. I want to allow it to remain mysterious and to delight in the breadth of imaginative ideas it evokes because what is revealed is Mystery itself—which is why I prefer to not analyze it. Nevertheless, I find Hillman's reading of it relevant, so I will include it here. He says: "The ultimate beauty of Psyche is that which even Aphrodite does not have and which must come from Persephone, who is Queen over the dead souls and whose name means 'bringer of destruction'" (Hillman, 1972, p. 102). Therefore, it is Psyche's task to know the beauty of death and to understand this herself. This is different than what Aphrodite can comprehend. Hillman (1972) writes:

> It is the beauty of the knowledge of death and of the effects of death upon all other beauty that does not contain this knowledge. Psyche must die herself in order to experience the reality of this beauty, a death different from her suicidal attempts. This would be the ultimate task of soul-making and its beauty—the incorporation of destruction into the flesh and skin embalmed in life. The visible transfigured by the invisibility of Hades Kingdom, anointing the psyche by the killing experience of its personal mortality. (p. 102)

This speaks to grasping the beauty and preciousness of life once we really become close to and experience the vulnerability of our mortality through encountering death. Aphrodite, as an immortal, can never relate to that beautiful fragility. Whether we come to know the mystery of life and death through grief when someone close to us has died, when we have had a brush with death ourselves, or when life as we know it has profoundly changed through divorce, for example. It is unique to the human experience to be able to comprehend the fragility and preciousness of being in a mortal body, and that is what also makes Psyche unique. This type of beauty is not available to Aphrodite—she can only get it via Psyche, because the soul mediates the beauty of the invisible inner world to the outer world of matter. Psyche relays the beauty of the inner psychic life to the outer, which is not knowable by the senses as is Aphrodite's beauty. Psyche is also the inner beauty that we intuit when we notice how someone glows from their eyes or their being.

What is it about Psyche that is beautiful? We see in Aphrodite sexualized beauty as she alluringly hides and reveals just enough of her voluptuous naked body to entice the imagination in Botticelli's "The Birth of Venus." But with Psyche, beauty is something else. It is not the adornments or accoutrements that belong to Aphrodite, and yet with both, beauty is essential to their nature. Recovering our sense of aesthetics is essential to a psychology of the soul. Psyche's beauty has to do with her humanness: her sufferings, her vulnerabilities, her embodied sensate experience, and her mortality. Her mortality reminds us of the fleetingness of our human experience. And what could be more attractive than a partner who can be vulnerable and delve into emotional depths? Through Psyche's essential beauty, we can appreciate and apprehend all forms of aesthetics, whether in nature and close to Artemis, or whether in Aphrodite and her sensibilities.

As the tale nears its end, at the point when she's awakened from the death-like sleep—after opening Persephone's beauty box on her return from Hades—we discover that Psyche is full of Pleasure. She's been carrying a child all along—the pleasure born of the soul. The first fruit of psychological creativity is pleasure. This promise of pleasure is what keeps us going when we're in the dark, decay of the *nigredo* experience, when things are falling apart and we are facing the four impossible tasks on the journey. It's necessary that we have hope that the other side of this is the birth of pleasure—the pleasure of living a life that is born of the soul.

There are two different processes at work in this: *consciousness* and *love*—love is where soul is made. To be in service to soul is to follow what you love—Psyche follows love, Eros. This is the way to guide our lives: follow what you love and you will live a soulful life, which will be a meaningful life that gives birth to pleasure. Consciousness expands consequently, as a derivative of living a soulful life. Hillman (1972) writes: "There is no real enmity between higher and lower pleasures or between one's work and one's delights, since the creative eros propels both" (p. 103). Pleasure is not restricted or confined to Aphrodite's sexual pleasure in the sensual world. In following what we love, pleasure is experienced in all areas of our lives, none being base or elevated, all being equally sacred.

Swans of Aphrodite

I became more curious about the symbol of the swan and wondered if there was a connection between Aphrodite and the swan as both serve as symbols of beauty, love, and grace (that thought had not occurred to me prior to this point). I found that the swan is one of Aphrodite's messengers and, in Greek and Roman art, she was sometimes depicted as riding on a swan. The bird's beauty and whiteness symbolize Aphrodite's grace and allure, making it sacred to the goddess. As Aphrodite guided

Psyche, she also guided the writing of this book in her own unique way.

I hadn't seen or heard much about Swan recently and began to wonder if I would. I had the intuition to trust the symbol, that it would continue to signal and inform me at the right time as a synchronicity, guiding my research on love. An old friend reached out and I was going to see him. He was widowed a couple of years earlier. We had lost contact over the years, and I was curious about what was at work in our reconnection. On the way, I felt open to a romantic connection if that energy was present, but mostly, I was happy to enjoy company with a familiar friend from my past and share stories. It felt like a call to adventure that I was delighted to receive (and the parallel with the swans wasn't lost on me). As I drove to the destination, which was a few hours outside of my hometown, wonder of wonders—there was a field full of trumpeter swans! There must have been 100 resting and preening in a slightly flooded field near the highway. My heart sang. I didn't think about what it might mean, marveling instead at the sight—in awe of seeing so many swans. Then I came across a second bank, about half the size of the first. Then a third further along. A fourth. And finally, a fifth group was within a couple of kilometers of our agreed upon meeting point! There was such an abundance of the great birds. I resisted the urge to seek their meaning with my mind and just basked in the feeling of joy, abundance, and affirmation that I was embarking on a call to adventure that was related to love. I hoped that maybe the lone swan I had seen behind my house had perhaps found its way to these fields, rife with similars, and likely companionship. I arrived and met up with my friend in a state of open-hearted joy. Our reconnection was as one might expect after the gift of seeing the swans—infused with romance, beauty, grace, sensuality, and a sense of magic that transported us to other realms. It was truly blessed by Aphrodite and perhaps even orchestrated by her.

In the days that followed, my heart felt large and expanded; the world had a new radiance. In fact, the season appeared to have even changed from the dullness of a long winter into a spring with early blooms. I was in the golden glow of Aphrodite. But this pairing was not going to work in the traditional sense, at least not at this time; that model was not going to fit our individual needs at the stage of life we were each in. Furthermore, Aphrodite's love is fleeting by nature. What lingered, though, was the experience of love that I physically felt in my heart. It was able to be expressed and directed to everyone and everything in my life. Love was all around. There was a sense of openness and expansiveness, and imaginings came alive with possibilities.

After being unpartnered for many years, I felt like I was entering a new stage. A stage of exploring and nurturing male friendships with the fresh intention of maybe choosing someone to partner with in a couple of years. I am self-reliant and comfortable identifying as a single person and feel close to the goddess Artemis, who remains separate from the world of men. I realized there would be more space in my life in a few years, but it seemed Aphrodite was letting herself be known now. Being unpartnered suits me as I love my freedom, autonomy, and sovereignty. I wondered if there could be a relationship that did not feel like it required the sacrifice of freedom. They are poles to be managed: freedom and autonomy on one side, companionship and coupling on the other. Freedom has been a paramount value for many years. But, a different notion glimmered through the week after the banks of swans and my romantic encounter with my old friend: the notion of a mature, secure-attachment with a partner. I had, at least, a revivified inkling of it.

Since he was in a nearly 30-year beautiful love story, I projected that he was capable and good at creating long-term, secure-attachment and being in a mature relationship. I didn't identify with these qualities in my life. Now, I know most people crave secure-attachment in romantic love, but as someone who is introverted, easily overwhelmed, has a lot of responsibilities, and knows the agony of various betrayals, I have not wanted a traditional-looking relationship in a very, very long time. In fact, I had worked so hard for my precious sovereignty, I didn't think I would ever consider it again. But here it was. I was unexpectedly considering the idea of creating a companionship—but only over a period of time, so as not to feel overwhelmed. Robert Johnson in *We* (1983, p. 196) had referred to companion-love as "stirring the oatmeal love" and I was horrified! That was 10 years ago—now I kind of like oatmeal and was willing to reconsider.

Reflecting on the paradox of freedom on one hand and being a couple on the other, I also recognize the familiar problem of the tension of opposites. Some of these tensions do not get outgrown, but require a conscientious effort to manage the balance between the two. Long-term partnerships necessitate an awareness of the paradox that we all carry, and the way to deal with it is to stay tuned in to oneself and speak up when more is required in either direction: more autonomy at one point, or more togetherness at another. But initially how to bear this tension felt like a bit of a conundrum for me. Here was this returning contemplation of companionship that I thought had sailed, that came along with a kind-hearted person entering my life. Neither of us were ready to create a committed long-term partnership, but we both wanted it within a few years. It all seemed odd. How could anyone really choose a partner without first letting themselves be seen and known, and vice versa? But neither of us were in a position to invest in "getting to know each other," due to geographical distance and responsibilities. Oh, Aphrodite!

"What is your biggest fear?" he asked me.

I didn't pause to think about it: "being seen." Losing my freedom is almost a tie. I don't have a natural proclivity for relationships, at least not at this late-middle-age stage in my life. Right up there with those two fears, is the fear of not fully living my best life. To me, living and loving is what it is all about. They are everything. In moments of clarity, I know that the purpose of my life, what makes it soulful, is loving—loving is what makes living meaningful. All expressions of loving: romantic, family, friends, home, nature, work, writing, breathing! So, I also didn't want to be missing out on living my best life by eliminating having romantic companion-love.

As a therapist, I know I'm not alone in this. Why is it so hard to let ourselves be deeply seen and known? It's a paradox, as it is a deep yearning as well as a deep fear. A few thoughts came to mind in this exploration. At the most basic level, it is the fear of rejection if the person does not like what they see. Rejection of our most innate being, if we were to really let ourselves be seen, would cut to the core and injure the most precious part of ourselves. Furthermore, the more important the person is to us the more the rejection wounds. There is also the risk of someone seeing something that we don't yet consciously recognize in ourselves. If something previously unconscious is identified and brought into consciousness, it will require the integration and reorganization of the identity that has been familiar and safe up to that point. In other words, it initiates a death and rebirth cycle and causes uncomfortable growth.

The fear of rejection is also related to the rejected shadow parts of ourselves. We have already rejected something about ourselves, and fear that someone else's rejection will confirm that which we've deemed to be unworthy of love in ourselves *is* unworthy of love. We must first integrate what we've rejecting into our conscious personality—all the stinking, smelling, foul, and shameful aspects of ourselves that we despise. Learning to love these parts of ourselves first, before expecting someone else to love them. Also, what is seen there might be the gold— the gifts we bring into the world—and stepping into that place of personal power requires self-agency, authority, and personal responsibility. Consciously, we might like how that sounds, but, especially initially, there is an infantile part of us that wants to be taken care of. Taking ownership of our gifts and strengths, that which we were born to do, entails a higher level of responsibility.

Of course, we can and should have boundaries around what we share with a partner and with the world, but the more intimate the relationship, the more those parts will be seen and exposed. We prefer not to have our rejected shameful parts come into view. This is seen in a funny-not-funny way, when women who have anxiety around relieving their bowels (behind closed doors) if they're within even-remotely-possible earshot of their beloved. This is an example of how we may not want a partner to be aware of our perceived-as-icky bodily functions, preferring instead to be seen as a radiant, sexy lover, basking in the erotic gaze. It is the first "I love you" moment when a woman reaches the stage of intimacy with her partner that she can allow her less attractive humanness to be acknowledged. She allows her beloved to acknowledge more of her whole being, rather than just basking in the golden light of her beauty. She risks breaking his fantasy projection on her of his idealized woman. Interestingly enough, this particular experience is almost exclusive to women. The majority of men are not all that concerned with their natural bodily functioning while in general proximity to their love interest.

As an alternative to romantic relationship, some will prefer to foster meaningful friendships while possibly also gently fanning the embers of love. This serves a few useful functions: 1. It allows people to get to know each other and be seen without the intoxicating complications of sex; 2. These friendships may be sufficient, as the desire for a traditional partnership may have dissipated; and 3. It mitigates vulnerability by not relying on one person to fulfill one's needs. If one is looking for a partner, having more than one option ensures that if one doesn't match, there are still other choices, which is a way around a scarcity mindset. Scarcity shows up in many ways: not enough money, time, work, and potential partners. "It's slim pickings out there," one client said—echoing the sentiments of many other midlife clients. It can feel like there are only a few swans to see, but there are many swans in the field, not just one in the slough. But finding them may require a willingness to venture outside the familiar and known. There are plenty of swans, even if some species are recovering from the brink of extinction.

Having friendships, even ones with romantic attraction, helps me stay in my heart and in the present, as opposed to getting 13 steps ahead of myself. The heady rush of the love potion has caused enough suffering in the past. Rather than seeing the person for who he was and what he could offer, I would fall in love with the potential that I could see in him. In terms of projection, this was also my potential. I would project it onto him and not get to know him as a human being, but rather what I perceived to be there—which was more about what was in me. And what I discovered was that my actual competency for forming a secure-attachment was probably better than I thought given my most recent strong projection was exactly about that. However, projecting does not allow us to be seen or to really get to know someone. It is useful for getting to know ourselves as well as the archetypes that live through us. If we want to have a meaningful human connection, we must allow ourselves to be seen and known, and we must examine what we are projecting and what we are genuinely getting to know about a person. Staying heart-centered means staying present on the journey and enjoying the love all around. Truly, what a fun stage of life to be at! And in many ways, isn't that always the stage of life we are at: enjoying the love all around us?

Incidentally, there was a beaver in the slough on the morning I wrote the previous section—time to get to writing. Usually, during big surges of creative work, I see the beaver toiling away on a regular basis; "busy beaver" comes to mind, among other qualities. Nature speaks to us like dreams; they both come from the psyche.

Sexual Desire

The conscious containment of our instincts as we move toward individuation is an essential part of personal agency and feeling in control of our own life. Instincts are linked to the archetypal sphere that emerges from the unconscious, and they have loud desires, drives, and appetites that can devour the conscious personality. When an instinctual drive or desire feels out of control, the rush or hot element that arises can be imagined as a flammable compulsivity. It is the experience of being in the grip of an instinctual desire and being possessed by it: we can get so excited by the object of our desire that we lose ourselves in the intensity. Think of the experience of falling in love; the intoxicating element that adds to the rush is this quality of overwhelming desire. In alchemy, we call it sulphur. Any form of addiction or compulsive behavior is also a signal that an accelerant is present. As we mature, the ego engages with these desires and impulses and thus transforms the compulsions, sometimes into emotions. The Self emerges as a result of this process. Without consciousness to contain and differentiate the compulsion, the ego will simply fall into unconsciousness again and the process will have to start over. To be objective about an instinct and its pull, consciousness is required. It takes a moral code or personal commitment to be able to exercise our power of choice rather than being swept along by instinct. A moral code standing against the instinct creates a tension of the opposites that enables the conscious person to make an empowered choice. I make it sound easy, but it is not. In reality, sometimes the best we can do is simply be compassionate toward ourselves while waiting for the archetypal grip to release us when it is good and ready. This seems to require an act of divine intervention or grace.

A person might be hooked in the same complex pattern for many years, conscious of it even, and yet no amount of will liberates the person. Sometimes if we can engage with the spiritual element through symbolic ritual we can make an offering that might be received. For example, one woman was in a 10-year pattern with a man who would vacillate between promising her the moon and then abruptly abandoning her for months at a time. This woman in midlife was conscious of the patterns, including her attachment wounds, and had tried therapy, love addiction groups, leaving the country for a prolonged period, and dating as a way of moving on. She tried a spiritual community, and then gave up drinking for over a year. She didn't identify as a compulsive drinker, but she was really out of options. It is hard to say if that was received by the gods and goddesses as an offering, or if perhaps a divine element finally took pity on her, but miraculously, the archetype driving the pattern released her. She met a genuinely stable partner who could appreciate her and, over time, they formed a secure, loving bond. The reason giving up alcohol is intriguing is that, on one level, it allows for clearheaded thinking and the steadying of emotions. But at a profound level, it is a tincture that is made from the essence of particular plants. We even refer to hard liquor as "spirits." There is an element of the spiritual in the tincture of alcohol. Also, alcohol is highly flammable, and maybe in her case it needed to burn off.

The compulsive element must be expunged from the desire, to reach the ideal condition of experiencing the instinctual longing, but not surrendering to it. We want to remain separate and objective so that we can activate the power of choice. We do not want to repress or deny our desires. We can learn to separate out the compulsive element from the full rush of the love potion, so the passion is not lost. Ideally, this is done with equanimity so as not to be thrown off balance. We want it to be expressed with control, safe in the knowledge that the destructive, extreme, possessive nature of the desire has been overcome.

One moral value that can stand against the rush of our instincts is respect. Notice what it feels like to share erotic intimacy with someone whom you respect and who you feel respected by—versus someone who may want sex to be transactional. Desire without respect can be a hot physical pleasure, but it can also turn sulphuric, introducing the element of compulsion that takes over one's conscious personality. Sure, it'll be spicy and fun at first, and you'll get a rush of happy brain chemicals (oxytocin, dopamine, and endorphins are all released), but with compulsivity, it can feel out of control, and feelings of shame, regret, or inferiority will likely follow within a few days—the shame-hangover. The need, the underlying need, is not being met. Conversely, when eroticism is shared with respect, it feels expansive, life-giving, and generative. Now here is the rub: self and mutual respect can diffuse the compulsive element that leads to increased authenticity and intimacy. However, it is also likely to require more emotional vulnerability, which is scary.

I wish it were not so, but as we allow someone to get closer to our authentic self, there is a greater risk of being hurt by that person; we bump into the whole problem of the fear of being seen again. It's not necessarily that the person would intentionally cause harm, but our experience of injury would be greater since it is closer to our essence and our feelings are greater and more genuine. As the conscious personality, the ego, is ever-ready to do its heroic duty to protect us, it will come up with all manner of ways to prevent such potential harm. That is when it becomes important to kindly self-reflect on: Why am I doing this sabotaging behaviour? What is actually going on? What is my deeper desire? Does this sabotaging behaviour support that? Can we stretch without forcing or overstretching?

Let's talk about triangulation—relationships where three people are involved. I'm not exploring infidelity here. That is a different topic. Infidelity is about a life that hasn't been lived or needs that aren't being met by an established intimate partner. "Established" is the differentiating word, where there is already an existing commitment or agreement in place with one primary erotically intimate partner. I'm also not referring to various forms of consensual non-monogamy as those agreements require a high level of vulnerable communication and self-awareness. Here I want to explore triangulation in the context of developing intimacy with a new partner where there is at least an initial indication of mutual respect and regard, but there is not an established relationship.

An anecdote will help: A woman describes an experience of newly reconnecting with a person she had previously known as an acquaintance, but life circumstances unfolded in such a way that they were both single and dating at the same time. He invited her on a second date and offered to cook dinner for her. She anticipated the coming dinner date with great enjoyment. However, on the day of the date, she became restless and slightly anxious. She felt tired and fatigued. But despite all that, she rallied up the courage to go, though she was aware of her vulnerable state, but reported feeling competent to manage boundaries to ensure actual safety. And still...! In order to protect her, the ego devises a "better, safer plan": contact a previous sexual partner, who is likely to respond happily to a booty call with no real intimacy. Her inner voices battle it out. On the one hand, it appears to be a good plan (trying to mitigate vulnerabilities). Though, rationally, she knows a booty call isn't what she wants, and she has long since explored that option with her previous sexual partner. Nevertheless, the urge to reach out to him increases as the dinner date approaches. She made a deal with herself that if she still wanted to connect with her past sexual partner, she would do it the next day, after the dinner date. She clarified her priorities, and reminded herself that she did not have the emotional bandwidth for drama and complications—and involving a third person would create both of those. "Do I really want to create drama and complications for myself?" she asked. She ended up getting to dinner without triangulating and she felt it was worth it, and did not reach out to the other man the next day.

So, what was going on here? This type of triangulation is for the purpose of protection from vulnerability and intimacy by calling in a familiar lover that won't fully satisfy emotionally. But it will feel good. Think of it as a safety net for a high-wire act. If the underlying desire is for an authentic experience of intimacy, the kind that takes courage to voice needs, wants, desires, ideas, hopes, dreams, and boundaries, then a safety net of a third person is helpful in not feeling so exposed and vulnerable. Creating a triangulation to protect against genuine intimacy, however, is antithetical to the deeper yearning. That is not to say that her dinner date would evolve into that, but on an inner level, it provided her the opportunity to develop a greater understanding of vulnerability and triangulation.

When the sexual instinct and its appetites are suppressed and then awoken, they can overtake the conscious personality in an aggressive manner. The task is to maintain consciousness in order to create safety for the more emotionally vulnerable aspects of the psyche and make choices that are aligned with personal values. If the ego falls into the unconscious and gets lost in the lustful desires of the drive, then the person may make choices that are not good for them, not good for their human life commitments. If Aphrodite is the goddess behind the sex drive, she isn't benevolent to the human condition.

Dream themes that I have had around the nature of the sex drive have included the symbol of a Pitbull, named Butcher, no less. *I knew Butcher from my past and found him in an old house I used to live in during my unrestrained 20s. I was happy to be familiar with Butcher and see he was contained in this old house, to which I held the key. The property was now valuable and was a bit of a hidden gem.* Butcher represented the animalistic and powerful sexual instinct, particularly at a younger age when that drive was active and unconscious in my life. I struggled with my sexuality in my twenties, and it appears from this dream, 30 years later, that I value this old house that is my body and I have control over the key to my sexuality. It was nice to see Butcher in the dream, though I had a healthy respect for him as a powerful animal. Animals in dreams often represent instinctual drives. I knew this one was about the sexual drive because of the events going on in my life at the time I lived with Butcher and at the time when I had the dream.

Another figure that has appeared that depicts the theme of containing sexual passions is the firefighter. One such dream occurred when I was experiencing a strong erotic attraction to someone and had a dream of a firefighter seeking me out to sit with me while I was feeling uneasy. There was a sense of safety with him, that he would keep things from getting away from me, or engulfing me. He was capable of containing the fire, so I could relax.

Sexuality inspires individuation as an instinct equal to the spiritual instinct, and it plays a significant role in awakening the ego to the Self. To put it another way, consciousness develops a relationship with the pantheon in the archetypal sphere through the psyche. The sexual instinct is not the only catalyst for individuation, but it is a potent one. Being in a relationship while individuating requires a reassessment of all our beliefs about sexuality and morality; what is true personally, and what is enculturated through a patriarchal lens. Each person must then learn to navigate the paradox of autonomy and togetherness, since they are individuals as well as individuals who are part of a pair—a single and a plural. Related to managing the paradox of I-we, there is also the managing and care of the relationship itself. We can regard it as its own living entity, and both partners must each tend it with love. We can see it as the space between the two that exists because the pair have come together; it is the eros that dances between them. We can take a break from analyzing and focus our attention on the mystery of the in-between realm.

The ultimate gold of relationship is in its very mucky struggles that we run up against with one another, as each effort we make enables us to blossom more fully into our own being. Of course, love is not *all* struggle; otherwise, we would never desire it. It is also the "divine ray" as Sappho (trans. 2002) wrote. Love is an archetypal experience that brings us into relationship with the transpersonal other; it can transport us into the realm of the divine—and it can transform us into humble-noble human beings.

By bringing our innate being out of the shadow and tending a conscious relationship with our instincts, we will be led to questions, and eventually our own answers, about our attitudes toward sexuality and relationships. Furthermore, the often-messy entanglements of relationships serve as a catalyst for deeper engagement with the wild soul; for example, when we are attracted to a new person after we have bonded with and committed to someone else, which is threatened by that attraction. Learning to make choices, rather than succumbing to the intensity of our instinctual desires, particularly the sexual instinct, is an essential step on the journey to wholeness. What better place to confront that most powerful of instincts than in the arena of romantic attraction. Indeed, as the most powerful instinct and drive, it is our work to learn how to co-exist with it, while honouring our human commitments and personal values. Repression of desires only leads to them overtaking the conscious personality—as the drive then operates in the shadow, giving it relative autonomy.

Following the quiet voice inside the body, the one that is of the soul rather than the loud ones of the instinctual appetites, will serve as a reliable guide. Maybe it does mean that the correct action, from the soul's perspective, is to follow the love feelings toward this new person. For a time, this may be impossible to assess for the individual, and each person's best answer is the one that feels most aligned with their personal integrity; not the moral code of the culture, but one's personal morality—which is revealed through holding this tension. For example, a man who was married for 10 years and had a child with his wife, developed feelings for a new woman. He wrestled with his conflicting options. Finally, he paused between the two women, and for the first time, he could hear the quiet voice within him, and he made the decision to follow his heart and embark on an unknown journey, but one that felt authentic to him. It was terrifying, but genuine. The morality of the heart is often inconsistent with the morality of our commitments, thus the ego, or conscious personality will feel crucified between the two poles. But if one can hold the tension, clarity will emerge. There isn't necessarily a right or wrong way, just different consequences to deal with responsibly. Following what feels true to the heart can create the life path, but that is likely to be messy and rife with internal conflict, as well as conflict with people we care about. Human relationships, and all the struggles that come with them, serve as a catalyst for the development of both self-awareness and soul-making.

Authentic sexual expressions are ever-changing and unique. What works for one person will not work for all, and what works for one person one time, may not work the next. This is true for many sexual issues, whether we're talking about orgasms or larger issues like sexual identity, which we now recognise is changeable and not constrained by binary or dualistic limitations. Sexuality is slippery and fluid by nature. It requires a constant state of attunement to one's body and soul. We want to strive to respond to each erotic moment, exercising our rights to assert or decline, or to explore or disengage, tuning into our feelings and somatic responses as a guide. Attunement to the body necessitates the separation of sexual appetites from subtler feelings and sensations. Those who struggle to remain present and focused for a sustained period of time would do best to simply slow things down—whether for a moment, a day, or a week. Our sexuality is ours to own, and we do not owe it to anyone to share it. The process of reclaiming one's sexuality liberates the individual's values from cultural ones. To have great sexual intimacy, we must learn to stay connected to our bodies rather than our minds. While fantasy and limerence, which are functions of the mind, contribute to foreplay, actual physical sharing requires moment-to-moment awareness of the sensory experience in the body.

The psyche and soma are inseparable, just as Psyche is inseparable from the human condition. The body asks that we recognize the undulating nature of sexuality and respond to each moment. The body is a physical expression of an individual's soul, which is connected to the anima mundi, the world's soul. As such, the body, like nature, speaks to us in symbols, synchronicities, and metaphors. I like the image of a glittering web to visually describe this. The web, we can imagine, provides vitality to each little glistening sparkle in it. We are the sparkles. Our personal, unique little sparkle is both *on* the web and *of* the web, and we all affect one another and are affected by the web. We coexist with the web and one another. I'd be happy to swap the word "web" for the anima mundi here. As we come into alignment with ourselves, then we can create purposeful, meaningful work—our personal soul's work—paradoxically, we come into service to the world's soul. Tending our personal soul, is also tending the world's soul, and that is the call of our time.

When women receive messages about their sexuality through a patriarchal cultural lens, they are more likely to accept that their sexuality is passive and receptive, that their bodies are receptacles inviting penetration and offering pleasure in exchange. When men receive messages about their sexuality from the culture, they are more inclined to believe that being assertive and domineering is the norm. The dominant cultural lens reflects only one version of sexuality, which is grossly insufficient. Collectively, we are working toward kicking the patriarchy out of its citizens' bedrooms and out of women's bodies. Patriarchal institutions should not have agency over decisions where authority, by definition, should belong to those who will bear the consequences. Etymologically, authority means being the author, leader, or master—we are each the authority of our own lives and bodies. It is up to each individual to make decisions around sexual identity, monogamy, polyamory, and abortion (to name only a few contentious issues). So long as consent is the determining factor in every exchange, at every step, these choices empower each person to live authentically.

Soma

Through socialization, many of us separate from our animal body and its wisdom—usually early in life and often as the result of some degree of trauma. Therefore, before we can hope to find our own expression of our personal sexuality, we first have to recognize that split and then endeavor to learn to hear, feel, and love our own body. The body carries the wisdom of the instincts; the wild soul communicates to us through our bodies and our dreams. Our bodies let us know when something just 'doesn't feel right.' But many of us are conditioned to ignore our body wisdom. We begin early on to discredit our instinctual knowing in favor of the mind. Rejection of the body often starts around puberty as a result of the messages we receive consciously and unconsciously from our parents and culture. At minimum, living in a culture that portrays Eve as the seductress and as responsible for original sin, most of us women have been wounded sexually; we received the confusing message that our bodies are both objects of desire and scorn.

Depth psychology recognizes that the physical body mirrors and effects an individual's psyche. Bridging the psyche–soma split by inviting a mature person to reconnect with the somatic wisdom is essential to mine the jewel of personal sexuality. The authentic expression of sexuality is felt in the body, and therefore we must strive to stay present in our home, our body. If we look to the soma as a messenger of soul in much the same way we would look to a dream, then hopefully, we can make choices that are in accord with a more holistic perspective that includes the embodied soul. Pain or suffering can be a doorway into a deeper complex, and each symptom can become a gift. Psyche and soma are inextricably connected, and movement at one level necessitates awareness of change at the other; consciousness then becomes grounded in praxis, and decisions are made from a somatically informed perspective.

An energy block or injury to the psyche may show up symptomatically in the soma and vice versa. Awakening awareness in the body where sensation has been split off from consciousness due to trauma or violation helps to dissolve the blocks; this reconnects us to the organic life of feeling and can help heal the split between body, mind, and soul. As we become more embodied and awaken our split-off parts, we actively reclaim our bodies as our own and are also actively engaging with the wild soul whose wisdom is known through the body. The mind and body offer different modes of wisdom, and both are required; the key is to differentiate their various modes.

Many of us sometimes find it just too emotionally painful to be present with the organic feeling life of the body. It takes tremendous courage to be at home in one's body and feel the full range of human experience: the love and ecstasy, the suffering and pain, and everything in-between. It is a challenge to reclaim the wisdom of the body. It is valuable to combine depth psychology with somatic work—such as yoga, or dance, or body work—so as to open and release blocked parts of the body and come to new awareness and understanding. Consciousness is required in order to understand the meanings of bodily experiences, and integrate psychological levels of the process. Somatic work paired with psychotherapy can provide insight and bring about a new perspective, which is required to integrate the bodily experience. Imagination and awareness can be helpful in discovering the meaning of a particular symptom and in providing a new attitude and perspective. Psychotherapy can assist and support in that important integration step so that what we gain does not fall back into the unconscious.

But do not be too concerned with seeking meaning at this stage. That dishonors the emotional, non-reason-oriented soul by being analytical, literal, and rational—relying on our logos consciousness for meaning. However, we can honor the soul's symbolic language—without rationalizing it—in our meaningful encounters with the numinous other that is embedded in the body. This is not easy, because we can slip into seeking clarity, but that is the ego's way, not the embodied soul's.

As we become present to the ever-increasing subtleties of the body, we are invited into a heightened awareness of the moment through movement, feeling, and sensation. It is a gift to be an embodied human; we are blessed to have this vessel to sense life. Somatic learning has the power to enhance the grace, beauty, and enjoyment of life. It is a birthright to enjoy life. When we come to recognize the gift of being in a human body, we can savor all of it.

Another way to reclaim the body is to work with dreams. Dreams are pure unadulterated voices from the autonomous psyche, and like the body, hold innate wisdom to which our conscious self may not otherwise have access. The body is always dreaming. One of the techniques I like to use is to embody dream figures. In doing so, we begin to build a relationship with dream images. A dream about a tree, for example, means to stand like the tree and feel its deep roots penetrating the earth and its vast branches reaching skyward while the strong trunk provides home and shelter for all the guests. To physically stand in the pose of a tree and feel its beingness in one's body is to relate to the tree in a new way, and we may find that from that tree, profound emotional strength is available to us that can hold all of our concerns.

Just a note of caution, however: this kind of work is best done in a supportive environment, because some dream images should not be embodied. These are powerful symbols of archetypal forces that are not all benevolent. We run the risk of overidentification with them or absorption into them if they are not related to with respect and care. Trust your instincts about which dream figures would lend you support and be helpful to relate to through the body. As we do that work, we affect the psyche, and conversely, as we work with the psyche, we affect the body.

Once we have made strides in inhabiting and reclaiming our body, we can move on to reclaiming our sexuality. This is not nearly as linear as I am making it sound; like all processes of the psyche, reconnecting psyche and soma will likely be circumambulating and probably disorienting. We can only strive to be present and aware of the body's messages. The quickest way possible to know what is authentic for each individual is through the immediate feedback of the body. However, not everyone has immediate access to embodied feedback because of confusing messages and past violations. Discovering one's own unique sexuality requires listening not only to the body but also to one's dreams and fantasies.

Reflection Questions

Jung suggested libido was a generalized psychic energy that could be used to motivate behaviors, including sexual, spiritual, intellectual, and creative ones. What are your thoughts on where libidinal energy may come from and what it can be used for?

If you adopt, for a moment, an Aphroditic perspective, available to all individuals, does that alter your exploration of libido? What is your understanding of the quiet voice of the body and the soul, compared to the louder voice of the sexual instinct and its sometimes-devouring drive? Have you had the experience of diverting your libido into a creative project, or into soulful endeavours that are meaningful to you? What is your experience of the voice of the instinctual sexual drive and the quiet voice of the soul?

Active Imagination Q & A

Question: I see libido as a natural force within all of life and, as a single woman at midlife, I find I prefer to express it in creative ways. I feel I have the energy to invest in creating my own life and I am excited about that; we can reach profound alchemical depths in our creativity. I am comfortable being introverted at this stage in my life. Is it possible to view this as the retrogression of my libido, where my focus must turn to the inner world? I see the archetypal longing behind our sexual longing as a longing for union with God. Is this one way that our libidinal energy can be used, to focus upon an ecstatic union with the God-Beloved?

Shelby: I appreciate how you are focusing on the non-sexual ways that libidinal energy can be experienced and worked with as a diverse natural force. It is a dynamic energy that never appears to be static or stagnant; it can move forwards and backwards, outwards and inwards, and can energize us for the enormous tasks involved in individuation work. It can also be used to sustain our creative endeavors, especially those in which we are deeply invested. Longing for another can be a longing for the spiritual or sacred. It is the spirit longing to reconnect with itself. This is the hook of projection, that we see the divine in the other. Some people's libido energy may need to be directed toward a spiritual practice for a period of time. Long periods of celibacy are well-known in most spiritual orientations. But we must return to the body and the human realm, to lived experience and relationships (though not necessarily romantic). Living a messy, full, authentic life is a kind of sacred devotion.

Question: The way Jung describes psychology in his essay does not fit well with the other sciences because there is always an ouroboric paradox of the psyche studying itself with itself in psychology, and thus the notion of quantifying the libido appears problematic. As a therapist, I noticed that there also appears to be a link between the severity of trauma and the severity of the resultant complex and pathology. Does this lend credence to Jung's thesis of libido equivalency, that the equivalent energy that disappears from our life in one form will show up somewhere else in our lives, either consciously and unconsciously?

Shelby: It is challenging to use empirical data in psychology compared to the other "hard" sciences. As a social/human science, it is different, and that must have been a difficult tension within Jung with his medical psychiatric mind and his irrational comprehension of the phenomena of the psyche. Of course, from the perspective of soul, the imaginal or mythical frameworks are best suited, since rationalism has separated us from the imaginal and it is necessary to return to the imaginal in order to reclaim lost soul fragments, both for the personal and the world's soul. Your thoughts on trauma are intriguing; this is an area that I am always interested in, especially as a clinician who tends to the trauma of the body and the soul. Many times, I am in awe of what some people have endured and how they have come out thriving. The inverse can be true as well, when someone's resiliency may seem to be under-developed compared to others. I wonder what it is that fosters resiliency. Is it related to libido in a more general sense? Perhaps it is transpersonal or generational trauma that shows up as symptoms. For example, if the personal trauma doesn't match the severity of the symptom, then we should look back generationally to see if there is an unhealed intergenerational wound. It is common that the person experiencing the symptoms carries the family's shadow. Hopefully, that individual can then be the chain-breaker, the person who breaks the chain of trauma and contributes to healing their ancestral wounds. That could seem to account for the different levels of resilience that certain individuals have. Resiliency appears to be developed by adversity, and thus, certain individuals and cultures with intergenerational trauma may demonstrate greater resiliency. Also, one's constitution will be a factor in both libido and resiliency: one person might have a delicate constitution, like a hummingbird, while another might be robust, like a buffalo.

Question: I think of libido in terms of kundalini, soul, Qi, or life force, etc. and equate both (libido and kundalini) with the essence of psychic energy. In my opinion, there is only one essential life force energy, which we can call spirit, and this spirit vibrates at a spectrum of frequencies, which includes the psyche and the body. These are merely various densities or incarnations. The kundalini, expressed as libido, can include a drive for materialistic desires like sex, money, power, and recognition. However, that same libido is also expressed at a higher level as other qualities, like creativity, love, kindness, insight, wisdom, and so forth. These energies are not better or worse necessarily; they are simply what they are. Do you think these parallels are beneficial ways of understanding libido?

Shelby: Thanks for sharing your views on libido or life force. It sounds like you don't quite agree with Jung's suggestion that libido is different than the "life force?" There is so much nuance in all these terms, and, of course, even more now than 100 years ago, when he was writing—before eastern philosophy was popular in the west. Your comment also got me thinking about the concept of spirit-in-matter and the personification of certain archetypal qualities that want to be manifested through the human experience. The idea was expressed well by Teilhard de Chardin (though it seems a bit unclear if it was him originally) that "we are not human beings having a spiritual experience, we are spiritual beings having a human experience."

Question: Can there be a quantitative measure of psychic energy? It seems that it is precisely this drive to reduce and organize psychic phenomena that, when pathological, only serves to remove one from the experiences at hand. If we use a mythic lens, are we better able to experience the sensory world and understand this energy through our bodies? I think I understand the difference between sexual desires and the quiet voice of the soul through my body. I might feel turned on and aroused by my partner. My body might respond to the stimulation at that moment and the desire could overtake me, but, then a few days later, I might have some sort of somatic symptom, an infection maybe—which tells me I need better sexual boundaries and that I have been ignoring some issues we need to address.

Shelby: I like your suggestion to stay with current experiences, which I would call staying with the human embodied experience rather than seeking spiritual heights. Your question about quantifying psychic energy is interesting. There is definitely a paradox at work in the psyche studying the psyche through empirical measures. Through an Aphroditic lens, we experience this dynamic and fluid energy, or phenomenon—we become the vessels through which it is expressed. Your grasp of the difference between sexual instinct and the soul's voice in the body is excellent. It can seem like everything is fine once the drive has taken over, but then the quiet voice finds a way to make itself heard. Mysterious somatic symptoms are definitely one of those ways.

Psyche's Third Task: Exercise

Psyche must collect water from the river Styx in a glass vessel. The river flows to the depths of hell and returns to the highest crags and down again in a circular fashion. It is guarded by monsters and there is nowhere to set foot near the edge to collect water. Psyche collapses, numb with defeat, when Zeus sends his golden eagle to her aid. The eagle takes the goblet, lowers it into the dangerous waters and safely returns it to Psyche.

The river is the river of life and death. It is vast. The task is about how to relate to the vastness of life and death. We can only do so, one goblet at a time. If we take too much, we risk being overwhelmed. This task is also about the value of the eagle's vision and getting a higher vantage point when we are too close to see the whole picture. The crystal goblet can be viewed as the vessel that holds the conscious personality, as the container of the ego. It is delicate. If it is inundated it might break. It is the container that holds the water of life. One morning, after a sleepless night feeling inundated with the too-muchness of my responsibilities, I awoke to a blanket of heavy wet snow covering my long driveway. One heavy shovel at a time, my son and I quietly dug out a path. As we finished the snow eased off and the clouds opened up for the sun to come through. I went for a walk on the trail behind my house to take in the beauty. Thinking, "What else should I have done?" Yes, there are a lot of pulls on me: tasks and people I care about, including my son, this book, and my clients. I muse about this and pause to take in the awe of the light on the snow-covered forest. "I am in the tasks now," I think, "they are teaching me how to live, how to find Eros." Then a full size, adult bald eagle flies right in front of me and makes a 90-degree turn to fly straight at me, low in the forest. "I feel you," I say to it. It lands in the tree in front of me, with the most dazzling light reflecting on the snowy tree limbs. I stare at it as one does when nature awes. Then it occurred to me, "Zeus' eagle!" Here I am in the third task—completely overwhelmed by the too-muchness of the river Styx, the river of life and death, and here comes the eagle, gifted by Zeus. I remember: focus, one task at a time, use eagle vision to select just the right spot (priority), then dip, and using care, take one goblet at a time—do one thing at a time and do it well. Just like my son and I shoveled, one heavy shovelful at a time, take on one task at a time—that's how it gets done. This is also seeing in double-vision, perceiving both the literal and the metaphorical.

Johnson (1989) suggests the third task is about doing one thing, doing it well, and in proportion. Many possibilities open up to us in life, and we must choose among them. We must be like an eagle, focus on a single spot, and then dip out a single goblet of water. "We can focus on one aspect of life, or one experience, concentrate on it, drink it in, and be satisfied. Then we can move on to whatever may follow in good order" (Johnson, 1989, p. 63). When the fragile ego is overwhelmed by the too-muchness of modern life, then it is time for eagle-vision to focus on one goblet, one task, one step at a time.

According to von Franz (1992), the river Styx, like the collective unconscious, cannot be grasped or held. She suggests that creative achievement is the only vessel which can hold the water of the Styx. Psyche is gifted the vessel through divine intervention, Zeus sending his eagle. At the moment when the human psyche cannot act by itself, it is supported by a heroic, intuitive spirit (the eagle) which arises from the unconscious. Psyche is saved by grace, because she has made a courageous and honest attempt.

Erich Neumann (1956) suggests the Styx is the stream of vital energy; the essential quality of the river is that it cannot be contained. Psyche's task then is to give form to that which is formless and flowing; as a vessel of individuation, she is ordered to siphon off a portion of the flowing energy of life, to give form to life. She has to encompass this power without being shattered by it.

Psyche's Third Task: Reflection Questions

As with the other exercises, journal your responses to the questions and share them with a safe friend or therapist. Where in your life do you need focus (one goblet)? Where in your life are you overwhelmed? Could you instead do one thing, but wholly and well to have a more meaningful experience? Where do you feel stuck, because you are too close to the flow of life? Where would eagle-vision help you? With eagle-vision focused on one task at the right place at the right moment, what do you see? What can you do to honour that? What is the next small step you can take? Where can you bring in the attitude of less is more, rather than more is better?

Chapter 6
Beyond the Romantic Tragedy

Let's check back in with the swan. Well, now I know the difference between a feral mute swan and a trumpeter swan. The swan I read about whose mate was killed in my neighbouring community was a mute swan, distinctive with an orange beak, and, as mentioned, invasive in Canada's natural habitat. The swan I have seen twice in Squamish is a trumpeter swan, with an all-black beak and it is the largest of the species in Canada. The local trumpeter swan is wild and native to Canada and was only recently brought back from the brink of extinction. The growing number of mute swans may impact the breeding success and population recovery of trumpeter swans in areas inhabited by both species.

I read that the lone surviving royal mute swan was in fact easily captured without incident by being corralled into a crate. Apparently, once in the crate, she sat and started preening, which indicates a calm, relaxed bird. The bird was believed to be the female of the pair and was described as "definitely feral, not at all tame." I like her! The experts planned on examining her, and taking her to the refuge where they would possibly try to introduce her to a potential new mate. But they noted that, sometimes, "animals may prefer to stay single." My projection plot thickened. I too love being a feral, single woman (and I love preening). The tension of opposites amplifies: my desire to be a feral, single woman on the one hand, and my desire to find a potential new mate on the other. What will be the symbol that will arise out of this paradox? Certainly, the swan is part of that. I believe that the story will continue to evolve. There is no update on the wild lone trumpeter swan at this point.

Explorations

This chapter examines relationship paradigms that go beyond romantic tragedy, and particularly beyond the suffering in romantic love—even though it can create a more soulful relationship with the world. We now want to see what's on the other side of this romance-as-suffering paradigm.

Let's return to the fourth task and Psyche's action of opening the cask of beauty ointment when she was forbidden to do so. Neumann (1956) referred to this as her "failure," which was also paradoxically her victory—it was a necessary failure for her to both know death and surrender to her feminine nature. This type of failure and surrender is contrary to the typical hero's journey of dragon-slaying and conquering. There is a type of hero's journey that Psyche goes on through all of these tasks and yet the way she accomplishes it is different than the masculine hero principle, which is the ego's way, and the Western psyche's way. She's travelled a sort of hero's path and developed skills, fortitude and consciousness, and yet, despite the warning from the tower, she opens the beauty ointment. This is a fascinating action because we would all probably believe that after the development she's done so far, she would know to not open it. Yet the 'failure' of opening it *is* her success. Neumann's (1956) suggestion is that the mortal Psyche is saying to herself: "My acts, my sufferings may move him, may force admiration from him, but soul alone may not be enough. Yet one thing is certain: no Eros will be able to resist a Psyche anointed with divine beauty" (p. 122). She thinks because she's anointed with the divine beauty ointment from Persephone, which the goddess of beauty wanted her to retrieve, that Eros won't be able to resist her. While parts of that interpretation can be somewhat inflammatory for us more modern women, we must remember to think of it as a metaphorical action on the internal level—Soul is willing to sacrifice everything for Love.

Psyche sacrificed her Eros paradise for the sake of spiritual development when she brought in the lamplight of consciousness and the oil accidentally dripped on Eros and woke him. In some way this is the sacrifice that comes with consciousness that enables psyche to evolve and spiritually develop through the tasks. We see this thread paralleled in the Christian myth with the garden of Eden story when Eve eats the apple because doing so is a necessary development. She must leave the Garden of eternal bliss to grow and develop. We find this same theme in Psyche's story, of needing to pursue consciousness and leave the Edenic stage of "ignorance is bliss," or the dark palace with Eros, in order to grow.

Here at the end, we see Psyche sacrifice again on the journey; she's done all three tasks, she's almost completed the fourth task and she consciously, knowingly, opens this jar of beauty ointment! In doing so, she is sacrificing all of the spiritual development that she achieved so far. She regresses into sleep, the consciousness she gained returns to the unconscious. But this begs the question: is this actually a regression? No. It is not a regression to the old matriarchal position, to her previous kind of unconsciousness. By preferring beauty to consciousness, she reunites herself, with her soulful nature; Psyche, after all, is the essence of human beauty. It is through Psyche that Aphroditic beauty finds its way into mortal humans. Psyche does this out of love for Eros. Her Kore femininity, the naïve young maiden, enters into a new phase. In pursuing beauty over knowledge and consciousness, she's reconciling with her own nature—she's accepting who she is, and her own kind of wholeness. The beauty she chooses isn't the attractiveness of youth, nor is it the alluring, carnal beauty of Aphrodite. "It is the beauty of a woman in love, who wishes to be beautiful for the beloved, for Eros, and for no one else" (1956, p. 123) as Neumann romantically puts it. Psyche has not become narcissistic. Rather, she has become herself.

We can view Psyche's failure as necessary. Von Franz (1990) provides an example of this in clinical work; she describes that toward the completion of analysis, after the hard-won struggle of developing consciousness has been endured, that dreams provide less and less guidance about what to do, what to figure out. Instead, it becomes more about just learning how to *be* in the world and to just live. She tells the story from Zen Buddhism, seeming to refer to the 10-oxherdering paintings which describe the process of enlightenment. The story is about an old man walking around with a beggar bowl after experiencing great enlightenment, "he has forgotten the gods, he has forgotten the enlightenment, he has forgotten everything. But wherever he walks, the cherry trees blossom" (von Franz, 1990, p. 107). This forgetting, or so-called failure, is not a regression to the previous unconscious state, it is its own type of progress. It's a progression to Taoist Uselessness, which is a letting go of the over-valuing of Western productivity. It is returning to a simplified state of "being" rather than "doing." There is less striving, hustling, and output of energy. At that point in therapy the whole intellectual aspect of searching for insight and for instruction from the unconscious, goes away to a great extent. "That would be the higher aim," (Von Franz, 1990, p. 113).

At this midlife stage that I am in, I find moments of this. There is a tension between wanting to simplify and live a quiet anonymous life, and a desire to scale up to have my work out in the world—so that maybe it finds some resonance with some

166

people; but my greatest hope is that it helps the world's soul. My stage of life is characterized by how to be creative for the sake of tending the anima mundi, while staying gentle and not hustling. I find moments of that sweet spot we call "flow state" while bearing the tension. Often that tension is somatically experienced as pain in my shoulders and it tells me when I am pushing too hard.

At the end of the Eros and Psyche myth we can view this type of 'regression' in Psyche's choice to open the box, which is one of the few choices she makes in the tale. We come to a point where we are so wholly ourselves that we no longer rely on rational thinking or analysis to figure things out. Taoist Uselessness allows for free and easy wandering, which means we align to the nature of things effortlessly and in a relaxed way—flow. But the old man with the beggar bowl in the 10-oxherding images did not start there. It is the culmination of the journey, as it is with Psyche. We flow when we align effortlessly. We flow by hearing and honouring the quiet voice that knows; she speaks in our bones, bodies, dreams, synchronicities, feelings, emotions, imaginings, and fantasies.

Psyche declares her primordial nature by defying all reason. She integrates her irrational underworld consciousness as a result of heeding her feelings of love for Eros. It is just this that causes the act of grace from Aphrodite who then forgives Psyche and allows Zeus to deify her. Her sacrifice for the sake of love is an act that renounces all logical values and throws caution to the winds, thus Psyche attains Aphrodite's favor and grace. It is Psyche's failure that has led Eros to intervene, which turns the reckless boy Eros into a man, and transforms the burned fugitive into a savior. It also allows Psyche to repair the betrayal that drove him away when she brought in too much consciousness too soon. (Though one wonders what would have occurred had she been able to hold the tension longer). She is prepared to give up her lamplight of conscious and go into darkness, for Eros. Through Psyche's sacrifice and death, the divine lover is changed from *puer*, eternal boy, to a man because in Psyche he finds something that exists only in the earthly human realm: rebirth through love.

In Psyche's apotheosis, Eros and Zeus, the King of Olympus, both honor the human soul, due to its superiority in love. By demonstrating her superiority, Psyche has proven herself to be as divine as she is human—which the gods now recognize. Our human capacity to love is our gift and blessing. Human loving *is* divine. In surrendering to her capacity to love, Psyche completes herself. She has gone from extreme activity to devotion. In doing so she calls forth the best of Eros. Love is the poison, and it is the cure. Love caused Psyche's travail, and her sacrifice out of devotion to love redeems her. Thus, Psyche's failure is the final assimilation of her true nature as the human soul. This extends beyond romantic love, and broadly to whatever it is that soul is drawn to and loves. The entire enactment of romantic love can be seen with double-vision on both the literal level and the symbolical level—soul seeks that which she loves, regardless of what that may be and she is willing to suffer and sacrifice for her love. The art is discerning soul from the instinctual appetites and desires of the archetypes, which can be loud, compulsive, and potentially destructive.

Now I want to explore some lived paradigms and alternative ways of being in relationship. Part of the problem, maybe the biggest challenge of all, is the way that patriarchy damages not only women, but also, importantly, how it damages men. Men who benefit from patriarchy may be inclined to cling to the rewards and forms of power patriarchy extends to them. This is significant for love, since they are not encouraged to be loving, especially older men. Since patriarchy wounds men in the place where they could be self-loving by imposing on them an identity that denies their wholeness, in order to know love, men must challenge patriarchy. And there are men who are rising to this challenge as allies. Such men are called to loving and wholeness because it too is an instinctual drive. These are the men that are really showing up by fostering their emotional intelligence and challenging the idealization of male aloofness. I see in my therapy practice truly brave men who are wanting an emotional connection and intimacy. They express the deep desire for wholeness in wanting to be able to experience and express their emotional life. Shifting the inner and cultural patriarch will challenge and change the way that men and women relate to themselves and to each other. These are the men who are willing to be challenged and they're willing to change, which also changes the patriarchal structures. There are all kinds of bumps on this road as we move along trying to define what the new masculinity for men should look like— both men and women are trying to find that. Women often send mixed messages to men and that's of course confusing, and so these struggles are prominent in the arena of romantic love.

Patriarchal culture is distinct from men/males: *men are not the problem—the problem is patriarchy.* It serves no one to contribute to divisiveness by blaming or shaming the other. If there is a direct and specific behaviour from someone that is causing personal harm, then assert and protect yourself with your voice first. If the behaviour persists, you will have to decide if you want to have that person in your life. This fosters self-trust. An important point to remember in connection with the fact that men are not the problem, but rather an overly-one-sided patriarchal culture, is that we have an inner-patriarch within us. We all inevitably do, just by virtue of living in a patriarchal culture that's been around for more than 2000 years. Western culture is built on the foundations laid during the Roman era, when it went from being a ramshackle republic to conquering the vast lands surrounding the Mediterranean Sea—thus it became the thriving Roman Empire for approximately 400 years. Colonization is steeped deeply into the psyche of patriarchal culture and reconciliation is required. We need to repair culture collectively, and we also need to do that individually. Since the Roman Empire is the foundation for white and non-indigenous imperialism, the inner-patriarch is deeply entrenched. The more we become conscious of the patriarchal water that we are swimming in, the more we can change how we inhibit in and change how we relate to others in our lives. It is not an easy task to identify all the ways patriarchal culture influences us, because we are so immersed in it. One route many people are following is reconnecting with their ancestral lineages and cultural traditions.

The path to self-love is arduous. We do this work usually by going back to childhood to reparent and love ourselves. We have to change the relationship to the inner-patriarch and matriarch in order to develop healthy relationships with men and women in our external life. Of course, there are other options that men and women explore such as same sex partnership, that won't alleviate the growth opportunities (challenges), but it is likely to reduce the problems related to a dominating inner-patriarch. Hooks (2003) also suggests revivifying "romantic friendship" as a viable option, which she describes as nuanced friendships that exist in any configuration of gender or sexual orientation. Such romantic friendships lack sexual engagement but they are rich in erotic passion. Non-sexual erotic passion has little meaning in today's world, so it's a revival of an old paradigm of friendship. It includes an erotic dimension to the passionate bond, which acts as energetic force enhancing and deepening ties between the two people. The difference from other forms of loving friendship is that both parties involved acknowledge the erotic dimension that acts as an energetic force in their bond.

The erotic is present, but not acted out sexually. We see this most successfully in situations with colleagues where the attraction gets transmuted into creative vocational work. It is interesting as a therapist how often we hear of erotic attraction developing at workplaces and how confusing it can be for many clients to just allow that without having it interrupt their primary commitments. Of course, it is not confined to work, often romantic friendships have deep roots and history and are mutually nourishing for both parties.

Hooks (page 172) also suggests a "circle of love" with committed bonds that extend beyond the privileged partnership. The circle involves nurturing multiple committed bonds, rather than only one. This likely includes deep romantic friendships even if there is a primary partner. Ideally, both partners understand the importance of sustaining committed bonds of love in romantic friendships. These are friendships with men and women, with commitments, which are consensual with the primary partner— they are non-sexual, even though there's an erotic tension. The sexual longing is not repressed, there is instead a choice to use eros as a basis for strengthening a committed friendship, similar to diverting libido the way Jung described—but for the purpose of fostering connections. Romantic friendships and a circle of love are a threat to patriarchy and heterosexism because they fundamentally challenge the assumption that being sexual with someone is essential to all meaningful, lasting, intimate bonds. Sex, then, is no longer the delimiter of a relationship.

Furthermore, removing sex as the defining attribute of relationships allows for a true expression of polyamory, literally meaning, "many loves," which expands the perspective beyond the monogamous, "one love" perspective. Each person can then experience love all around them, but may still choose to be sexually intimate with only one person in this model. It allows for a both/

and experience of polyamory (many loves) and monogamy (one lover) if that model aligns with the individual's values. It means that a couple doesn't have to fulfill all the roles and be all things to each other. Hooks (2003) also points out there is a problem with the word "romantic" friendships, since within patriarchal culture "romantic" evokes the possibility of sexual activity. But if we can embrace that term, while developing non-sexual bonds, we can build relationships that will last a lifetime. As polyamory in all its expressions is rapidly becoming the model of choice for many people, there are almost as many models of that as there are couples. Some people are "poly" and single, maybe with a circle of love and lovers with whom they share close bonds. Some people are "poly" but not experiencing deep intimacy, these are sometimes more "casual" relationships. Other times there can be a deeply felt connection, but only for a fleeting moment. Some couples who have to be apart for long periods create agreements that "whatever happens" during that defined period of time is acceptable, and they probably don't identify as "poly," but enter into the category of "consensual non-monogamy." There are countless variations of consensual agreements for navigating such boundaries that are suitable for both people and their soul's needs. Consensual non-monogamy is increasingly popular, though many people are less concerned with what the structure is called and more concerned with how to talk about alternative paradigms and needs with their partner.

Celibacy is a self-loving choice for many people who prioritize building a beloved community. Such people are free to lead joyous lives as single folks; and sometimes, if not always, as celibate folks. "Celibacy is often a liberating self-loving choice among women for whom the search for sexual pleasure has constantly led them down a self-sabotaging path" (hooks, 2003, p. 224). It can be empowering to choose celibacy consciously in order to be self-loving, while maintaining a circle of love. Women with a history of sexual victimization find celibacy a better alternative than joyless sexuality that is not life-affirming. A circle of loving relationships mitigates the risk of loneliness. Celibacy in this context does not have to be a life-long commitment, and one doesn't even have to identify as a celibate, it just might be what unfolds. It can change, as can any of the paradigms suggested. It also does not have to be a spiritual asceticism that denies the body and pleasure. Celibacy doesn't entail giving up on love at all, instead it can be a way to bring loves into someone's vocational life.

As women sacrifice the patriarchal fantasy of rescue—the Oedipal fantasy of all-powerful parents who take care of them—they achieve their greatest freedom, personal salvation. They no longer need to believe that someone else will save them, and instead can become sovereign over their own body and life, saving themselves. Women then shift their energy from looking to manifest love in a conventional way, to sharing it in other ways, such as how they are in the world, or in their work. When this occurs, usually in their 40s and 50s, women gain a sense of what they can do in the world and are freer than ever—free to do all kinds of work, free to find each other. Love comes as we find love within.

To risk self-knowledge is to begin love's journey. As we get older and wiser we come to love ourselves and our life more. In doing that we change our relationship to love and to what we are seeking; disillusioned by and liberated from the knight in shining armour fantasy, woman are no longer seeking a hero or savior. We turn our search for love into a grand life adventure and a profound spiritual quest. We find we love being alive and in loving living. Once liberated, we are free to manifest our greatest creation, an inimitable life. Along the way, we do find soulmates, true friends, life companions. We find loving relationships. No matter how sweet the love between two people, we ask too much if we demand that this relationship with this one other person be everything. The truth we hold close is that *love is everything*, and because love has this power, it is always there within us and within those we love. It offers us the possibility of ongoing intimacy.

Approaching the Fourth Task

As we approach the fourth task, we can wonder if everyone goes through this process of individuation at midlife, because really, who would voluntarily trek off to Hades and back? The depth psychological approach of honoring Jung's process of individuation takes courage. Some simply must do it; the price of ignoring the soul's call is far too high. Others seem to be able to avoid the path of individuation and transformation—and, who can blame them? The path of individuation is not for the fainthearted. *Living*—fully and really living—is also not for the fainthearted, because living means feeling the full range of human emotion, coming to accept all of who we are: shadow and all. It means coming to accept others and their so-called imperfections too. It means accepting that, like life, we are perfect in our imperfections, quirks, nuances, sufferings, moods, hurts, and so on.

Not everyone would agree that we can avoid the call, but argue that we can only anesthetize ourselves to it by clinging to certainty, medications, and intoxicants to put off answering it. To heed the call means we must endure looking at all of who we are and learn to sit with all of what we feel. We cannot only become receptive to light, love, peace, pleasure, and joy. It seems that the further we are on the journey, the more chaos and paradox we have to become comfortable tolerating; at least initially, it is the chaos that deepens us into a soulful engagement with the world—later we become aware of what is happening and that makes it easier.

Typically, we go through individuation around midlife as a result of some sort of crisis, or something that completely changes our world view. Childbirth can be a catalyst. While it is regarded as a joyful experience, the transition to having a dependent is a dramatic reorientation of one's values and perspective. Because of the tension the catalyst will cause, the transformation process will be initiatory. We become disillusioned with particular cultural messages we have believed were our own, such as the fantasy that marriage will make us whole and complete. We begin to wake up to what we thought was ours, only to become unsure and unclear. Our personal values start to percolate and challenge cultural values. And our personal values might be in conflict, tearing us apart, dismembering us from the inside out, so that eventually we can re-member who we were born to be—re-member our birthright. The process requires us to assess our own personal values, ideals, goals, ethics, and integrity. We must make the descent into our depths to discover the verities of soul, beyond any cultural tenets.

Reflection Questions

The myth ends with the conjunction of love and soul, the reunion of Psyche and Eros. What pulls you in about this? Reflect on how this might be enacted in modern times: psychically with the inner Other, and also in modern relationship with the partner. What would it mean to retain consciousness while being engaged with Psyche and Eros in the arena of romantic love? Is that possible and/or desirable? Is it possible that "conscious" and "unconscious" are terms that become too dualistic and rational for explorations pertaining to soul and love? In addition, reflect on the development of the masculine principle as seen in Eros through this myth. What might it mean that Eros is mostly absent and silent throughout the myth? Finally, please comment on your thoughts regarding the influence of patriarchy on the paradigm of romantic love and the alternative relational paradigms that appeal to you.

Active Imagination Q & A

Question: I found Psyche's journey, as a myth of individuation and totality of Self situated in the context of Western patriarchal culture, intriguing and relevant to both men and women. Do you think the "marriage of death" is an apt metaphor for the ensouling experience of the *coniunctio,* whether as an intrapsychic union or conscious lived reality in one's relationship? I do not necessarily want to construe the lived reality of relationship or marriage negatively, like a literal death; nevertheless, there are experiences of *la petite mort,* the little death in relationships. We experience the death of our conscious expectations and unconscious projections rooted in the world of consciousness and its values.

Neumann (1956) wrote, "Feminine individuation and the spiritual development of the feminine . . . are always effected through love" (p. 110). At first, I did not agree, but then remembered that it was heartbreak that brought me to my first analysis. However, dreams soon brought me past that into self-love, a relationship with myself and to the way the sacred manifests through me. I had always avoided this by giving myself up to romantic love. Do you see self-love as a way to become balanced, and engage in a conscious relationship with spiritual or archetypal forces led by the animum that calls us to integrate the inferior function?

Shelby: I am again reflecting on the longing for romantic love as being the symbolic longing for the inner *coniunctio*—longing and heartbreak are the catalysts for the journey. The myth may leave some with an unresolved tension between Psyche's desire to become conscious and her desire for erotic love—these can seem polarized at times and I think there is an opportunity to move towards a both/and to overcome the tension. For example, to become conscious and desire erotic love, rather than favouring one over the other, creates a tension to manage rather than transcend. Jung was an advocate for consciousness as the purpose of a human life; but for those of us who resonate with the Eros and Psyche myth perhaps it is both consciousness and love, including self-love, and the myriad expressions of love. The myth is about expanding consciousness from the moment she brings the lamp in, through the tasks, and until she regresses into "unconsciousness." Then she re-awakens with a new consciousness. All the tasks are about increasing consciousness in ways that are fundamental to the human psyche, but all for the purpose of reclaiming love.

This last task points to a need to surrender to the god involved, in this case, to honor Aphrodite, from within. Psyche's surrender to beauty is just as necessary as the work of expanding consciousness that we see in the first three tasks. Prioritizing erotic love, symbolized by Psyche's desire to be beautiful for her beloved, is also necessary for feminine spiritual development. Psyche's curiosity to know the goddesses, to know what's in that box, which is after all the journey she is on, is her strength. Her human vulnerability is her strength, it is not weakness or failure as commonly understood. At midlife, this may be experienced and expressed inwardly as self-love, which is also led by the animum, and need not be an erotic love with another, or maybe it is with many others, but the boundaries rest with the individuals to create and navigate.

Here's an additional musing on the connection between love, grief/death, and soul. The degree of grief corresponds directly to the degree of love. The anguish of loss, such as Eros' flight, or in whatever way it shows up, is a doorway to soul. This may have something to suggest about the Mystery of the box. In the pain of her grief, Psyche looks into the box that she recovered from the goddess of the chthonic underworld—the kingdom of the dead—and thus becomes the deified soul. In opening this box, she gains the knowledge of the beauty from Persephone's realm. There is, as you suggest, a correlation between marriage and death, seen both in the beginning of the tale when she is sent to wed death, and at the end when she opens the box.

Question: Psyche's failure of the fourth task is a regression of libido; her energy has gone into the unconscious. Thus, it is a progression in her life whereby she sacrifices consciousness for beauty, and a quality of Aphrodite emerges. Aphrodite is no longer the dragon of the traditional hero's journey to be slayed, but rather Psyche is to win her over by surrendering to her values of love and beauty. I don't believe that conscious and unconscious are too dualistic for soul and love, but that the *coniunctio* of these two psychic fields are joined in the nature of love.

Instead of romantic relationships, are some people called to conscious relationship with archetypal inner experiences that can help them develop their inferior function of thinking or feeling? Even if they long for romantic love, do you think some people are nevertheless compelled to set out, alone, on Psyche's journey toward consciousness and toward a different manifestation of Eros—embodied more by the first three tasks? On the other hand, at times, it does seem that, like Psyche, we embrace Aphroditic beauty over knowledge, when we honor Aphrodite from within ourselves. Is it better to neither privilege beauty nor union with Eros through romantic love as the only path for feminine spiritual development?

Shelby: I suspect Aphrodite would approve of being honoured as an experience to be embodied, rather than a dragon to slay through accomplishments and clarities. I also like how you are

178

in essence suggesting that the third thing, or the transcendent function, between conscious and unconscious is *love*. The dim light of consciousness must resonate in the body and the soul must be aligned with beauty itself—something unconquerable and only to be experienced.

We can look to the other manifestations of the archetypal feminine figures for perspectives and myths pertaining to spiritual development—for example, Athena, Artemis, Demeter, and so on. Each person's psyche will have many that are available at any given time and each has their own myth and characteristics. Depending on what we are developing individually at any given stage in life, different archetypal figures will be predominant. While I was in school, Athena and Artemis were dominant. Artemis has been dominant the longest in my midlife journey, and she has required a lengthy period of aloneness and radical confrontation with the inner wilds of the psyche. Perhaps ironically, I am writing about Aphrodite because she is in my personal shadow and my creative life is her way of being expressed—so she doesn't go into a wrath. My love affair is with the imaginative work of writing. For people engaged in the rigors of graduate school, Athena will be strongly activated as the goddess of education, intelligence, and wisdom. The myth of Eros and Psyche is about the development of soul, thus it is a foundational myth for the human experience and specifically the field of psychology, which originally meant "the study of the soul."

Question: Do you find this myth frustrating, like I do, perhaps due to being situated within patriarchy? It suggests that only through Psyche's relation to various masculinities, in extremis and otherwise, that she develops. It struck me that while this story is compelling for various reasons, I have to question whether it can be included in the canon of Greek mythology as such, or whether it amounts to essentially Greek-myth-fan-fiction because it is a story written within the context of a novel.

Shelby: Thank you for articulating your disquiet about this myth. Your point is well taken that for the feminine to develop it is through the acquisition of what we associate with masculine traits. For example, the task of collecting the ram's wool is associated with the power-drive and aggression, if we consider those typically masculine traits. Also, let's not forget, the tale is embedded within the context of Apuleius' hero's journey. Your questioning of the context of the story is important; I might suggest that the bigger question is about the nature of the romantic love paradigm itself as that is what the story reflects. Whether we consider the tale a novel, myth, or fairy tale, is a bit of a moot point, as the nature of the model of romantic love in the West is reflected in this story, as is the nature of the relationship to the psyche, and the anima mundi. In addition, it has stood the test of time, thus it has become mythologized within the collective Western psyche. Thus, we find our way back to the notion of the colonization of the psyche in men and women, the collective, and in the anima mundi. We can also posit that the expression of romantic love is a patriarchal, colonized model of partnership. Once we are conscious of that, we can "decolonize" ourselves from that embedded social structure and relate to ourselves and each other in a new way.

Psyche's Fourth Task: Exercise

Psyche must journey to the underworld to fetch a cask of Persephone's beauty ointment and bring it back to Venus without opening it.

As with the other tasks, it is impossible for mere mortals to accomplish these without divine intervention. In this task, Psyche goes to a tower intending to throw herself off in defeat. But it is this very tower that comes to help her. It is not a creature of nature—ant, reed, eagle—instead it is one made by culture. The tower instructs her on where to find the pathless way leading to the palace of Hades; she must earn her passage with two barley cakes and two half-pennies in her teeth. It will take sufficient fortitude as the way is not without a price and requires preparation. She descends to the river Styx and encounters a lame man who drops his load of sticks from his lame donkey. In her kindness she begins to bend to help him. However, she stops because she has been forbidden to do such things, as it would exhaust her energies. Then she comes to the ferryman, Charon, with his patched boat; he requires one of the coins for passage over the river. While crossing, a drowning man begs for her help, and she must refuse him! She must save all her resources to face the goddess of the underworld and not be concerned with lesser tasks. Her next challenge is facing the three fates of the underworld, who are weaving the strands of fate on their loom. They ask Psyche for help. What a temptation! But again, she must pass them by. She is warned that she will lose one of her oatcakes if she doesn't, and she will need it yet. Next, she is confronted by Cerberus, the three-headed guard dog of Hades. She tosses him one of her oatcakes, and while the horrible beast fights with his three heads over the cake, she is able to pass. Finally, she is with Persephone. She was instructed by the tower to remain humble and refuse the lavish hospitality Persephone would offer. She accepts only simple food and sits on the ground to eat. Had she accepted the luxurious offerings, she would be bound to the palace of the underworld forever. Having gained strength and wisdom, she asks for the cask of beauty ointment, which Persephone gives without question. Thus, Psyche begins to make the return journey. She buys her way past Cerberus with the second cake; pays the ferryman with the second coin. But. But. The last of the instructions—"do not look in the cask containing the mystical secret"—proves too much. When she is within sight of the upper, human world, she succumbs and opens it. And she finds Nothing in the box! But the Nothing overtakes Psyche and she falls into a deep and deadly sleep, laying as a corpse. This inspires Eros to free himself and rush to her aid. He awakens her with the prick of one of his arrows. Psyche takes the cask to Aphrodite and completes the fourth and final task.

As previously noted, this is the task of "learning to say no." The task offers up all of the temptations that Psyche must resist, including her own kindness and compassion, and her own fate. She must not allow herself to be imposed upon or diverted from her goal or task. The tower is the symbol of introversion. With such a challenging task ahead, one is invited to withdrawal into one's own inner world for self-contemplation. It is through this withdrawal that Psyche is able to gather the strength and wisdom she needs to complete the journey ahead. The demand to avoid giving aid to those that ask it of her in the underworld pertains to knowing which things within the psyche are no longer in service to it, and need to be cut off and allowed to die, because they have outlived their time. Charon as the ferryman within the unconscious allows us to crossover from one conscious attitude to a new one. The lame old man called Orcus, meaning hesitation, who again and again winds up a black and white cord is the next figure Psyche encounters. Von Franz (2001) unravels him as the symbol that ultimately amounts to indecisiveness and not proceeding forward. People with a weak ego-consciousness and feeling function cannot take responsibility for their decisions, this indecisiveness lames them and they do nothing. The secret is to say, "to hell with it, I shall do *this* because this is me, and I am ready to pay for it; everything is half-wrong anyhow, whatever one does" (von Franz, 2001, p. 128)! *To hell with it!* Just choose what is authentically you and work it out. That is integrity with oneself. We have to allow ourselves to be conscious of ulterior, half-unconscious motivations and walk past them. Regarding the beauty ointment, von Franz (2001) states that it was not for Psyche to open nor to know of divine beauty, and the ointment would not have rendered Aphrodite unconscious; however, Aphrodite could not journey to Hades and back at all. It is clear that Psyche had to open the box, otherwise Eros would not have come to free her—just as Adam and Eve had to eat the apple for higher consciousness to evolve.

Reflection Questions: Exercise

What challenge resonates for you in this task and why? Can you think of examples of these challenges in your life? Where in your life would you benefit from saying "no" so that you can refocus your energy onto your life? What do you think of the notion that the box contained the secret essence of the feminine, and so must remain mystical? What would that be? What role do you see consciousness playing in this task? What would it mean to become too identified with Persephone? Why must Psyche restrict her qualities of kindness and generosity? Where do you see that you might reserve your resources better? Do see Psyche regressing into unconsciousness by marrying on Olympus? How can you honour and embody divine beauty in your life?

Chapter 7

Love of Soul

For the conclusion of our journey we are going to look into the notion that Psyche's journey towards Eros is sacred work. Love of soul is the work that awakens each of us to our inner vitality; it makes us come alive and feel excited to live our unique self-expression. Following our purpose means to follow what enlivens us, and it is unique for each person. One person will tell you he secretly would like to have his own painting business, another that she wants a food truck, another that he wants to fish. Whatever your secret love might be, follow that. It will lead you on the journey. We are all needed and we each have a place of belonging. Some will want to partner, some will not, and it will ebb and flow. For those in midlife who are sovereign and do not need a partner, they may still feel an instinct to partner, or not, and it too may ebb and flow. This is all dynamic because the life-force is dynamic, thus we are always invited to be responsive and adaptive to the moment.

We spend so much of our lives yearning for something, but we can't quite fathom what it is. So many of our apparent goals, and the things that we think we want, turn out to be masks for our underlying desires; they are symbols for our true values and qualities. Our deepest wants are not reducible to physical or material goods, or even to a physical person; they are psychological characteristics such as love, truth, honesty, loyalty, and purpose.

We crave something beautiful, valuable, and deserving of our devotion. When we attempt to reduce everything into a desire for a tangible object such as a home, a vehicle, a better job, or a human being, it never works. We are, without recognising it, seeking the sacred. The sacred, on the other hand, cannot be reduced to anything else and it too is seeking us. As a result, we may understand our longing for romantic love as a symbolic desire for connection with the sacred. Paradoxically, genuine loving acceptance created in mature partner-companionship can be sacred practice.

Quite late into writing, I became aware that this book is not about romantic love after all—at least not literally—it is about soul-making. Soul speaks to us in metaphor and symbol and romantic love is symbolic of the *coniunctio* between love and soul. In some ways I knew that in the beginning, and eventually the knowing settled deeper into my heart. When I started writing, I resisted letting this material really work on me: "I've been teaching it for years, I'll be able to write about it and be unaffected. It'll be *easy*," I told myself. If I hadn't believed that, I wouldn't have started. How naïve was I to think I could write a depth psychological book on a myth and be unaffected? (The innocence of Psyche at the start of the tale).

Late in the process, at the end of a complete draft, a mentor pointed out I was not fully giving myself to the work. I was crushed. I knew it was true. Then I had a dream. *I am with Mr. Miyagi (from the movie Karate Kid) and he tells me: "you have to go back to the beginning, back to the basics." I have two polishing gloves: "Wax on. Wax off."* I awoke from that dream, shaken to the core, but also, it felt right—heart and soul were present and I become intimately related to the material. The polishing gloves were symbolic of a substantial review and rewrite of the material. I had to go right back to beginning, back to the basics. Then I was open to soul's affectivity and love. I surrendered to the process and let the work have its way with me; that is the soul-making process.

Explorations

In this concluding chapter, "Love of Soul," I want to provide a synthesis of what I hope you take away from this book. The myth of Eros and Psyche on one level addresses the external world of lived relationship and human experience. But on another level, it reflects a sacred, psychological journey toward love and soul. The psychological journey is about falling in love with one's human soul and the human condition—more specifically, falling in love with one's sacred life.

The imagination comes from soul; therefore, we want to relate to the imagination without our ego's assessment and limitations and instead be curious. Hillman (1989) suggests that we *stay with the image* and remain curious about what the soul is doing within the image. Whether the image is from dream, or in a fantasy—wherever it's presenting—stick with image and watch the phenomenon. We want to try to avoid interpretation and only observe what the image is doing. As soon as we assume we know what the image is about, we are applying ego consciousness to it. But if we stay curious and observe we can learn much more about psyche. If you look to the images, they show where you are with your personal soul. Look at your dreams, daydreams, fantasies, reveries, synchronicities, etc. When you have an image, that tells you where you are.

Once we have an image or a figure we can build a relationship with it by communicating with dream images rather than interpreting them. Hillman in an example has described an anthill, and rather than interpreting the anthill with the ego as in, "my life feels busy and chaotic," he suggests observing it. Look at what the ants are doing, be interested and pay attention. This level of attention is quieting in itself. In being present with the image, we honour its autonomy. Again, the key is to not interpret, but observe. He furthers the example of the ants starting to crawl up the legs. We can say that "makes me crazy." But that is interpreting it. Instead, what can we do in relationship to the ants?

> I can brush them off, I can run around in circles. I can get a dish of honey to attract them elsewhere. I can sing them an ant song. . . . But what I don't do, won't do is interpret the ants. You saw that move—"They're crawling up my legs. I'm going crazy"—that shift from image to interpretation—and *that* makes you crazy. (Hillman, 1989, p. 76)

It is not so easy to be objective and not bring in our subjective interpretations. But curiosity and quiet attentiveness in observing the image will help. This allows us to be in relationship to psyche and where she is at. In doing so, I find sometimes we just wake with an inspiration, knowing what needs to happen; something has moved in our relating with the images of the psyche and suddenly we are impelled to move as well. Clarity comes through patiently attending the psyche, but not by egoic interpretive moves.

We can do this with the body as well. For example, I had been tending a strange body pain that I associated with too-much-busyness, not enough Taoist Uselessness. Then I woke up (having forgot the dreams), but understanding that the pain was due to "busting at the seams." That was the phrase I awoke with. Somehow that set about making space in my life, many small decisions that amounted to more roominess, less busyness. It wasn't interpretive. At that point after staying curious for months about the pain, suddenly there was clarity.

The etymological origin of 'therapy' comes from *therapia* in Latin and it means to attend, to make well; therefore, the psychotherapist attends the soul, or is meant to. In our tending of soul, both in a clinical context, and in human relationships, we find our way to relate to the soul, pierce through the veils that cover the soul, where we can see our very lives as the enactment of our dreams, as in a theatre. Here things get blurry around the question of what is more real? And who is dreaming who? If the ego allows the soul to lead by tending the imagination and soma, then suddenly we awake one morning with a new clarity. From Hillman's perspective, soul is *not unconscious*, rather *we* are unconscious and our task is to stick with the images of dreams rather than making interpretive moves which depotentiates the imagination. In tending soul, we are paying attention to the imaginal aspects of our life. In doing so, the inner world not only takes care of itself and its crises, but it also takes care of you, and your ego-worries and demands.

In tending soul's images, "one feels lived by imagination" (Hillman, 1989, p. 86). This is similar to a sentiment that Jung expressed, "it is not I who lives, it lives me" (cited in Wilhelm, 1931, p. 131). This is also where *Tracking the Wild Woman* concluded: that the wild woman—that authentic, innate, embodied soul figure—was, in fact, the one who was tracking me, even though initially (and for most of that research) I thought I was researching her. There is a perspective shift that happens as we come into relationship with the psyche, or the soul, and with the autonomous figures within. We recognize our external life, and conscious personality, are not driving. The "I" is co-creating with psyche by ensuring we're pointed in the right direction. But the deeper impulse comes from imagination. A meaningful shift in life that occurs when we are no longer in service to the ego, but to something deeper.

The shift begins with a kind of "psychological faith" that allows us to love the images that flow spontaneously from the psyche—recognizing that psyche communicates to us in reveries, fantasies, reflections, imaginations, dreams. If we move towards those images with curiosity, we build trust in the irrational way of relating to the world. If not, we stay locked in our problems and the ego's literalizations. This creates a sense of being trapped in material reality and a separation from the imaginal and daimonic, which is where we are moved by love and inspiration. "Lack of psychological faith is compensated by exaggerated personalizing, a fantastic need for people (and a need for fantastic people)" (Hillman, 1989, p. 86). We essentially project or transfer, depending on the context, onto other people the imaginal reality that is going on within our psyche. However, if we were related from an internal perspective and recognized psyche as an autonomous reality, and validate it, then we no longer get stuck in the literalization of that reality in the external world— we liberate ourselves and the soul. Importantly, it doesn't mean that we find a truer relationship with the soul by eliminating the person who we are projecting or transferring onto. We cannot eliminate the human that carries the projection or transference; in fact, we need that person in order to have that mirrored back to us—it's a phenomenon that occurs, regardless of whether or not we are conscious of it. There is no "what to do," there is no "essential formula," either internally or externally, we are just to recognize what is occurring.

Soul is tethered to life in the material world. It can't be separated from the body, from family, from its cultural and ecological environment, from mortality. Soul is about being in the human form, in life, engaged with our bodies, with our human experience, with our relationships. In contrast, spiritual efforts, which are also important;

> Focus their attention on afterlife, cosmic issues, idealistic values, hopes and universal truths. They try to perfect the body with yoga's and diets and demanding exercise routines. Spirit is to be found not only in church but also in the gym, on the corporate ladder and in higher education (as cited in Hillman, 1989, p. 112).

Spiritual pursuits tend to turn into idealistic perfectionism, whereas soulful pursuits are embedded in the nitty-gritty, messy entanglements of life where we are experiencing all of our embodied human affects. We find soul always in the thick of things, in the repressed, in the shadow, in the messes of life, in illness, and in the pain and confusion of love. Spirituality often seeks to transcend these lowly, uncomfortable conditions of the soul. It's easy to find ourselves spiritually bypassing and trying to avoid all these discomforts of being in the human condition—even though we may be unconscious of that desire to bypass. This movement—maybe we call it the New Age Movement or the Self-Help Movement—can be harmful to soul because it is pursuing something that is idealistic, or is an unrealistic ideal of perfection.

We want to foster awareness of the marketing and societal messages we are exposed to as these are industries that are embedded in a capitalist economy that must sell ideals to us as consumers in order for the economy to thrive. To the degree that we are able, we want to bring consciousness to the reasons that we might be pursuing something. For example, I love fashion, specifically, I love style as a form of self-expression. I also like feeling financially stable and these two things can be in conflict sometimes as fashion can be expensive. So, I get curious about the symbol at work in my admiration of style. I don't want to interpret it, but to stick with the image. Over the years reflecting on my long-standing love of style, I have gleaned a few things, which appeal to my ego, which likes clarity. One is that fashion is modeled on anima figures, it is a way of seeing a personification of psyche. Another is that fashion represents a persona, or mask, in which psyche is envisioning who I am becoming in the outer world, as she becomes ever more visible to myself and others. Another is expected, my ego simply likes the satisfied feeling of an outfit that makes me feel confident and myself. Yet another layer is that Aphrodite is largely dormant in my life, not by choice, and fashion can be a way honouring and tending her. I hold all of these semi-consciously, and balance my choices against my other human, adult values and priorities, without neglecting or shaming this valid aspect that also needs attention. Of course, material things are not a substitute for soul, nor is my love of style a justification for the rampant consumerism that is devouring our planet. We can tend the images and fantasy without enacting the other aspects that might be harmful. For example, we choose to buy what we need and have enough, not excess—we might fill virtual shopping carts or scour our favorite online stores, but we don't have to click the "buy now" button. We can choose quality or beautiful items that are imbued with soul over quantity. We can choose to buy used items and donate others that we have outgrown. Find creative options to manage the tension between consumerism and tending soul and the earth.

Tending our images and dream life with curiosity allows for soul to be our guide for navigating life when we feel lost. If we are in service to soul, we will find it in our ordinary lives. Life with soul is filled with felt experience. The movement of soul is downward into life, rather than moving upward toward spiritual perfection. To be in service to life and in service to soul, we move down and into the body, and into our human experience. That does not mean we move away from spirit or religion, it means we balance spiritual pursuits with soul, by fully leaning into life and imagination.

Soul, as Psyche, has a certain vulnerability and inferiority—it is found in hidden recesses, in the margins, in the marginalized— and in imperfections. By contrast spirit has an eternal purity and perfection. Ego, the sense of conscious identity, needs to be strong enough to engage with the archetypes without being shattered—staying mailable enough to allow for the imaginal to be lived through one's life. The soul's inferiority is one of the pathologies that brings us deeper into her realm. The spiritual is closely equated to the over-rationalization of Western culture and is balanced by soul-making. We need a sense of personal fortitude to hold these tensions, which a healthy ego can provide. For people whose sense of individual identity is fragile, these archetypal forces that break into consciousness can entirely take over the personality so that the individual then speaks out of the archetype and can no longer discern who they are or which reality they are in. This would be how I would describe certain psychiatric conditions such as schizophrenia or paranoia. With a robust sense of identity, or ego container, we can safely engage with the archetypal others, because we know where we are and which reality is consensual, and most importantly, we know the way back. A strong ego allows for the ability to move in and out of different realms. In living a life in service to soul one most surely feels lost sometimes; however, as the relationship flourishes, faith and trust build.

Culturally in the West, and maybe all patriarchal cultures, for many millennia, we've lived in pursuit of spirit. Because of the patriarchal system, this pursuit has translated into religious endeavors. As a counterbalance to that, we must move closer to soul, closer to the body, closer to the human experience. It is a time for finding where the pendulum wants to land individually and collectively in terms of balancing spirit and soul. If we aren't conscious that we are looking through the lens of spirit, then we may undervalue and repress life. Whereas if we can shift our perspective to be more balanced, or even move it toward a perspective from soul, we can come to appreciate living, really and truly living, into life and all that we can experience. Living is sacred. We don't try to transcend suffering any longer, we can be grateful to be right here in the muck of it. That would be the alchemical salt.

> Salt is the mineral substance or objective ground of personal experience making experience possible. No salt, no experiencing—merely a running on and running through of events without a psychic body. Thus, salt makes events sensed and felt, giving us each a sense of the personal—my tears, my sweat and blood, my taste and value. The entire alchemical opus hangs on the ability to experience subjectively. (Hillman, 1989, p. 125)

Being with our deep hurts, rather than treating them as wounds to heal, allows us to mine the salt to gain precious material that is nourishment for the soul. This allows for a new perspective on living a meaningful life.

In a previous chapter we discussed alchemical sulphur. We do want to differentiate salt from sulphur. Sulphur, in alchemy, often embodies the compulsive rush of desires that can overtake the personality. That's an experience that belongs to the archetypal drives and appetites. The soul's voice is imaginal and quieter, felt in the salty experiences of our blood, sweat, and tears, as opposed to the exciting rush of desire, the sulphur. Desire can be applicable to romantic love as lustful feelings, but really it can be in any type of desire that gives a rush. Optimally, we want to have the desire, but we want the compulsion to burn off symbolically. If you think of lighting a wooden match, the igniting element is the sulphur, the initial exciting flame, but that burns off quickly and the wood catches and burns comparatively slowly. We need the ignitability of the sulphuric element to get the flame started, and perhaps we light the lamp, candle, or cookfire, or relationship, but we don't want to light match after match until the box is empty. Perhaps then sitting by our candle light, we can allow the quiet voice of the soul to come forward.

With sulphur, the heart's desire and the object that is being desired become inflamed as one. We lose contact with our soul in those moments. The sulphur enthusing one's being is necessary, but it comes at the expense of the soul. It's a compulsive projection that can't differentiate the desire from the object and also can't hear the soul voice at that time. This is like the symbolic green lion in alchemy that dissolves the sulphur and devours the sun (the gold). It is necessary that the sulphur is burned off to discover the philosopher's stone within the gold. We have to be able to quiet that sulphur and let it burn off. We learn how to hold the tension of both desiring and to see through the desire at the same time with metaphorical vision. We don't want to repress the desire. Optimally, we can be conscious of the experience of sulphur and desire, while also reclaiming that energy as imagination. We can enjoy the juicy rush of an erotic, sulphuric enchantment, aware of what is happening and that it will burn off. It is, after all, one of the very pleasurable experiences in life, but this is different than acting out of compulsion, which is a willful leaping into the life experience presented, knowing the soul experience might lead to messy entanglements.

Ultimately, love is an initiation of the soul. All the struggles and longings involved with love are invitations to come into relationship with soul. In doing so we deepen into our being that is right here, grounded and engaged with life. As we build faith, we don't seek or require understanding of the processes and mysteries that are present in soulful love. Love that leads to psyche is not bound by human concerns and conditions. It is both active and receptive. It comes into life as grace, so that, like Psyche by the end, one has a relationship to love itself. From the perspective of soul, through the travails of loving, ultimately, what we come into relationship with is love itself. Love and soul are inseparable and they are the culmination of the journey.

What soul loves is love, what love loves is soul. Love is initially seen though our cultural lens, but if we look through the lens of soul, she is pursuing love, and that doesn't always, or often ever, have anything to do with the personal or the human commitments that we make. Where deep intimacy and connection is, soul is, and love will open. Love is always there, ready to be revealed. It isn't dependent upon a certain someone, it is dependent on what soul loves. If we live life in service to soul, we live life in service to love, the love that is always there. That doesn't necessarily have anything to do with human love and commitments, that is a different kind of love all together; maybe soul is part of that, certainly at first, but then maybe it evolves and soul needs other ways of loving.

Soul loves creating. Think of all the images that she creates every night in the dream state, drawing upon limitless options and pulling them together in her unique way. Anyone who works in communications, marketing, art, music, or any of the creative fields, knows how the psyche just goes on and on infinitely creating. Now if we sell-out her creations without engaging enough of our own soul or love in the work that we do for money,

196

something happens to redirect that use of our soul energy. Burnout, physical ailment, something disrupts the profiteering of soul's creative work. It has to contain love. We have to love what we are creating, including in relationships, or the soul's creative vitality gets exploited and will eventually wither.

As much as I am a romantic and devoted to soul, my lived experience has not included a romantic relationship that endured beyond 10-years. Nevertheless, long-term partnership can also be soulful. The challenge is to have an ongoing, intimate life with another person at the same time as we invite this unpredictable depth of soul into our lives. The solution is for both parties to respect soul, to acknowledge the mystery that is inherent in soulful life and to come to treasure that unpredictability. To do so entails a radical shift in values and a willingness to allow ourselves and our partners to be transformed. If we can keep the larger picture in mind and honor the tendency of soul to move in mysterious ways, we might see that the unpredicted developments that come from the soul can have a positive effect on a relationship. This offers continuous deepening of the connection and a grounding of the attachment in soul rather than in any one person's will, or cultural precepts. Besides, individual willfulness is usually laced with fear and manipulation, and is hardly solid ground for the building of intimacy. Couples can feel secure and still allow each other freedom to have experiences that deepen roots in the soil of soul. There is a tension to be cared for between freedom and security, and both individuals must tend that in the living dynamism of the relationship itself as the container of the pair. By being "free," I mean free to continue the ongoing journey of becoming one's best self and living one's best life, free to be seen and accepted by their partner with proverbial warts and all. By "secure," I mean having trust that you and your partner are secure and together, that you can weather life's storms. You know that each is an individual and you're both willing to talk and engage in respectful dialogue when soul presents some unexpected raw material. There is a deeper security when the individuals are rooted in soul. One knows that come-what-may, you will be fine, and eventually flourish—this security comes from having an established relationship with soul. From this deep security, there is less fear and clinging to the other person. The partner no longer symbolizes safety and security, that comes from within; therefore, both are freer to be themselves.

Even in couples that foster respect of soul, self, and other, there will be betrayal and hurt, there will be mysterious experiences that call one along the soul's path. Through the betrayal we can expand, and we can arrive hopefully at knowing the experience of forgiveness, which would remain unknowable without betrayal. A friend of mine once said, "sometimes stuff happens"—her and her long-term husband both had the ability to be securely attached to one another by being forgiving of their human transgressions, neither abused this. This couple didn't consciously articulate honouring soul in their relationship, but in their actions and attitudes they did. They had the ability to allow the other to each be themselves and to flow with the surprises that might arise which were in contrast to their commitments.

Each relationship has its own cultural elements. "The union in a marriage or a friendship is not simply the togetherness of two people, it is also the mixing of their background qualities" (Moore, 1994, p. 239). These can be shared by way of traditional rituals, stories, foods, creative works, and so on. At the family dinner table, soul may be more satisfied with attention to the way we eat and the cultural fantasies surrounding the food. Soulful life is intimate by nature and close to the home, family and heart. In addressing the need for attachment Moore (1994) writes, "If we're interested in living a life of attachment and desire, it helps to have bodies around, and the vernacular life is an embodied one" (p. 241).

Soul in relationship also comes up as ritual events such as anniversaries, birthdays, and other revolving dates, including certain moods and rhythms of closeness and distance that come and go. The soul doesn't move in a linear fashion, but themes ebb and flow, and then return again. Relationships have seasons to weather. Differences between people may give more to a relationship or friendship than what is held in common, precisely because the soul is so unique. We do well to have a receptive attitude and learn how to make adaptations to be flexible through growth and change cycles and seasons.

If we give attention to the way we express ourselves with our choice of dress, language, manner, and in doing so offer favor to beauty, then we are tending soul. The sterile conversations diminish and the soul creates its own solution. We evoke soulfulness by thinking and living metaphorically. The life of soul is the raw material that goes through a process of refinement. This applies to a romantic partnership, friendship, or even a new job. Everything starts out looking just great, "prospects are high," then in a relatively short period of time we are involved in the other person's soul stuff, the swamplands. Soul-work is the long process of taking the raw material of life, then making something of it. The raw material is the *prima materia* in alchemical terms, it is the grit and the stuff we reject and it can be found everywhere in our human relatedness. Soulfulness and intimacy in relationship do not come ready-made, it is through the process of refinement that they become valuable. The early attraction might be an intuition of promising possibilities; however, it is still only raw and unshaped. We let it work on us and we work on it by offering it our interest and curiosity. Joy or Pleasure is discovered in taking this raw material and making sparkling gems and tapestries out of it. If we can understand that soul material is given in its raw form, then we might be better able to forgive ourselves and others for not being quick to handle relationships with grace. From that perspective, we can see that the person is not being malicious, but that the stuff of soul is given in lumps that require sorting, shaping, refining, and even transmuting, all operations in alchemy. If we consider the relationship as a work of art, we can patiently allow it to reveal itself to us as we sculpt and refine it. Soulful intimacy is not found in clean, well-structured, meaningful, unperturbed, ideal unions—that type of idealism belongs to the cultural exemplar, hemmed in with a pristine white-picket fence. But once that illusion breaks down, we might find soul has other intentions, or rather, soul's intention causes the disillusionment.

Living with soul intimacy is not a step-by-step path and soul will often thwart ego's goals. Rather to live soulfully, "we allow hope, faith, and love to be open-ended; we do not know what to hope for, may not believe in any particular thing, and will love whatever it is we receive" (Moore, 1994, p. 252). Of course, this last part is not always easy, nor is it something we can willfully effect. We have to be willing to step into the unknown, trusting that it leads somewhere, even or maybe especially if it is irrational. Do we invest in a new education, a new career, a new person? These can require giant leaps of faith because of the unknown. I once was working as contract writer for a government organization's internal communications department. I was so excited when they posted the job as a permanent position—it had great benefits and security. I was devastated when the manager gave the position to a friend of hers. I moped through my final two weeks, scared of what I would do next since I didn't have any savings. My first day after I finished, I was sulking at home, fearful, and I got a phone call inviting me to a different department to write for them. The pay was much better, the people were more aligned, and the hours were fewer. With that position and freedom, I was able to make a move to a small mountain town and commute to the city only two days a week. It was a dream. Of course, way-leads-on-to-way, and eventually soul had a new direction.

As another example of courage, a colleague who had her own business for years, a yoga studio, began to feel out of alignment. She planted a few seeds, and rapidly it sold. She had no idea what she was going to do next. Soul's way led her forth, to a new business aligned with her ancestral roots where she thrives and supports people traversing their dark nights. You've probably had, or at least know people who've had, experiences of letting go of false security, only to find something better appears that enriches life even more. This takes faith and trust in soul.

We fair well by embracing paradox, because then we are no longer in the either/or mentality where things are this or that and clear-cut—which both the mind and ego like. In so doing we find ourselves breaking free of cultural norms. Soul-making is a radical departure from modern notions of living correctly and successfully at all levels: moral, spiritual, psychological, social, and vocational. But retrospectively, we may perceive a subtle vein of wisdom and benevolence. This has been my experience, though it is usually with hindsight that the wisdom glimmers through, and it is not to say past hurts don't cycle around again. In the final paradox, if we want to light the fires of intimacy we have to honor the soul of the other, this is not a surrendering to another person, rather it is respecting the soul in the other.

Human intimacy and its entanglements are essential and inseparable from soulfulness in all our relationships: parent and child, partners in marriage, friendships, or more distantly, co-workers and colleagues, neighbours, and favorite baristas. It is through these mysterious intimacies that we can experience the divine. Divine intimacy is inseparable from our day-today relationships. Our task is to be open to this dimension and its presence. The gift of being mortal, like Psyche, is that we have finite bodies that can sense, feel, live, and be here with each other. It's a gift to be embodied and to be engaged with all aspects of the human experience, some of them being quite gritty at times. Loving is the doorway to the divine, the sacred, eternal aspect. Recognizing the value in the struggle is about becoming more soulful. Soulful loving involves setting aside some of our ego's wants and goals, and our mind's logos consciousness and just being able to be in the thick of the rich vibrancy of life. The winding path to divine love and union is found through our vulnerable, beautiful human love and intimacy.

Reflection Questions

Please journal your reflections on the notion that the struggles of romantic love can be the container for transformation and contribute to the process of individuation. In your evaluation, please consider, what might be the value of the struggles with romantic love. Please synthesize what psyche (soul) and eros (love) means for you? What does *love of soul* mean, and from that orientation, how might that impact your relationships? Please comment on the notion that engaging in human love is a way of demonstrating love of soul and is sacred practice.

Active Imagination Q & A

Question: At the beginning of our relationship, our human love was deep, intense, life-changing, true love, but at its end, we had done so much work together that the gift we gave each other was the freedom to be with soul. We each went on to have other relationships, but even today we both find ourselves still choosing love of soul expressed as creativity over human beloveds. As Moore also noted, "Relationship to the divine . . . satisfies the soul in ways that no substitute can touch" (1994, p. 258). For my ex-husband and I, we wanted divine love more than we wanted human love. Is that the paradox you're describing, that leaving relationships contributed more to my individuation than staying within them?

Shelby: I appreciate your astute personal clarity around your values and priorities that you've gained in reflection, though it sounds like it was also conscious while you were in it with your ex-husband. The goal is not really that important (i.e. to stay together or not), but rather the experience itself is what matters as that is where soul is made, particularly with love. It sounds like love of soul led you towards beautiful love experiences and then back to creative life, more enriched.

Question: To me psyche or soul means the path of the self towards the spirit or Self, and eros or love means the fire of the heart that fuels the journey to get there. I think we see that in the way Psyche's love is the fuel that keeps her going, even when she wants to give up. Is it possible to see Eros as coming to her aid through all the helpers she receives, so that although he is invisible, absent or has gone dark, he is still there for her, helping her in a way only a divine being can? Love would indeed seem to be the fuel that helps power the individuation journey together or solo.

Shelby: Loving care for others is ultimately meant to help us grow as people and make us more conscious. Love and relationship empower us by enabling us to "know thyself" (as the oracle of Delphi instructs) through the mirror of another soul. Romantic relationship becomes about companionship on the spiritual path of individuation, and about closeness of hearts on the pilgrimage towards liberation. It is through relationship one is able to get to know one's self through the other as a mirror. This does take perseverance and dedication to bring more love and compassion into the world, in whatever form.

Question: I find my partner relationship forms a container that can hold the projections and transferences, as well as the conflicts required to transmute the *prima materia* into the inner gold of reclaimed psyche. Through this process, the interpersonal gold of recognition of another human being is slowly unveiled as layers of projection are shed. We have our own nuanced way of relating, as all couples do, and our private inside comments, jokes, and looks. Do you think a pair bond has its own private world that the outer world may only glimpse, but never know? Is its sacredness built on those shared intimacies?

Shelby: I love how poetically you describe the intimate and private living container of the romantic partnership with the inside jokes and shared experiences that only the dyad understands. It is a unique world that the pair create. It is also the container of transformation, beyond its special sweetness. Eros coordinates inexplicable synchronicities that bring us potential partners; compatibility is such a mystery. Sometimes that prick of Eros' arrow might be hitting the wounds in another and can become devastatingly toxic. Love is unconditional, but relationships require conditions, known as boundaries, demand work and contain deal-breakers.

Question: Love works on the ego in as much as it welcomes the provocations down and into that which is not yet surrendered. Do you view this as a necessary and sometimes painful awakening to both the self and other in the cosmic field of love? Are love and soul the culmination of the journey?

Shelby: Love does belong to the psyche not the ego, and in fact, the ego often has lots of desires and resistances, which serve to increase the alchemical nature of love. Through that we find ourselves in the alchemical process of soul-making. Through this journey we do come into relationship with love itself. We are the vessels of soul-making and from this perspective can observe relationships as alchemical and love generating fields that transform us individually and change the world.

Beauty "Let the beauty we love be what we do": Exercise

For this exercise, I would like you to read the poem by Rumi, "Let the beauty we love be what we do," and then review the reflection questions and journal your thoughts and responses.

> Today, like every other day,
> we wake up empty and frightened.
> Don't open the door to the study and begin reading.
> Take down a musical instrument.
> Let the beauty we love be what we do.
> There are hundreds of ways to kneel and kiss the ground.

Rumi says we start off each day empty and frightened. We resort to books, even holy books, to find meaning, love, and a sense of safety that we're longing for. However, there is another more spontaneous way: play a musical instrument, sing a song, create something beautiful. Rather than looking for beauty outside, or in a metaphysical realm, look for it in our actions, in our daily life. Enact the beauty that we love. There are many ways to find the deep sense of meaning, beauty, and love that we enjoy. Remember, beauty is part of Psyche's essential nature. For Rumi, beauty was the goal of the spiritual life, and love was the path that leads to it. Similarly, what we love, we find beautiful. Rumi is telling us that there are many ways to experience this love, this beauty.

Beauty Reflection Questions

What is the Beauty you love? What ways do you kneel and kiss the ground? What ways do you celebrate Beauty? What does Beauty mean to you? What is your relationship to beauty and the sacred life? What does that mean for you? What beauty does your soul love? How do you or can you express your beauty?

Conclusion

I began this manuscript with a hefty imposter complex, after all, I had been unpartnered for 12 years—who was I to write about romantic love? Shortly after the first swan appeared, there were the many swans that followed, and then the romantic experience after seeing the groups, or banks, of swans. Some weeks passed after this romance initiated, and the writing of this book concurrently proliferated. Our feelings blossomed, so we decided to meet again. Again, I saw two large banks of swans resting and preening in fields. My journey was far into a new part of the province I hadn't been familiar with as an adult; like going deeper and deeper into the psyche: across mountains, rivers, bridges, and eventually to a large, but rural H-shaped lake. Down narrow winding roads I went, to a driveway with a grand timber archway, which upon crossing, felt like the mysterious doorway of Narnia. The beauty of the estate was mesmerizing with its living log homes, immaculate landscaping, with just the right amount of wild, and a gently wind-blown lake. My romantic friend greeted me and for another three days we reconnected and basked in beauty and sensuality. Having known each other for over 30 years, there was an ease and comfortability with ourselves and each other that was uncharacteristic in any of my previous romantic encounters. There was also a degree of openheartedness that I have not felt before. In one of the many magical moments, we went fishing and I caught a fish. I have only fished a couple of times in my life, so it was both exhilarating and disturbing—I was concerned for the fish, even though I am not a vegetarian. My friend freed it gently from the hook, and I was able to hold its little body and allow it to glide out into the water. Some things are not meant to be caught and kept. Maybe most.

On reflecting afterward, the time together felt like it was graced by Eros and Psyche. It felt sacred, like love and soul both acted through us. "Follow, Pleasure," I kept hearing. We both felt a bit stunned afterwards, "what just happened?" In the week that followed, I struggled with conflicting feelings. I wanted to be able to continue as lovers and see if it would evolve into a longer-term partnership. I wanted to hold on to it. He knew he wasn't ready for a relationship for reasons that were easy to understand. I grappled with it internally, then prayed for clarity. I had a dream that revealed that I was too vulnerable in this situation and needed to be more self-protecting. I let him know, and he was worried about the same. At that point we decided to see if we could find a new rhythm of friendship and remove the romantic component. I prayed for guidance again, wanting to find the gold in this encounter, since I was writing about romantic love.

I had the following dream: I have completed a tour of a museum-type complex, a company that owns many different businesses. I and my companions go back inside at the end of the tour, through the exit door, to go to the gift shop and I intend to choose a souvenir. The company is most famous for zinc, there are many trophies, accolades, and samples of zinc. I dismiss the zinc, and find trinkets of gold. I peruse the gold, and none of the tiny trinkets are valuable. I decide to pass and we all leave. I awake. On waking, I rejected this dream. Where was the gold, the meaningfulness of the romantic encounter with my friend? I could see I had been in an old (museum) complex from the language in the dream. What do I know about zinc? Not much— sun block? Too much solar consciousness—could I be thinking and analyzing too much again? Probably. Another friend reminded me that zinc is also used for bolstering the immune system, it is a helpful mineral that reinforces our self-protection system. That resonates. I had expectations that it was supposed to be gold, but maybe the value was the encounter itself, not what I go back inside to find afterwards. It also resonates that the protective element was enacted when I listened to the dream telling me I was too vulnerable. The company I was in was famous for zinc, is that my own company or is that my companion-company? Both? Am I famous for self-protection? I don't think so, I like to think I'm open-hearted with good boundaries. I wouldn't say he is known for being self-protective either, I would equally say one of his strengths seems to be open-hearted kindness. But who knows, projection, and all? Maybe the psyche was self-correcting as it does.

I google zinc and find: "Zinc has a self-healing mechanism in it. The zinc coating sacrifices itself slowly by galvanic action to protect the base steel. This sacrificial action continues as long as any zinc remains in the immediate area" (Galvanizeit.org). There are times to be vulnerable and brave, and there are times to sacrifice and protect ourselves and not intentionally put ourselves in harm's way. Maybe the zinc was my psyche's self-protective barrier preventing me from being burned and corroding. The gold that I went inward to find after the fact was a trinket. That leads me to the thought that the experience itself was the gold, there was no souvenir to memorialize it or carry it forth. The experience of open-hearted loving and releasing was the gold. There is no trinket from the gift store to represent the fleeting Beauty that we shared.

Then a couple of months later, as this dream continued to bounce around and resonate with vitality for me—and after I finished 30-days of zinc lozenges—I had the thought, *the horrible thought*—maybe there was no gold because I was not brave enough to be vulnerable. Somehow that also felt true and accurate, as though I had failed to actualize the gold—as though I had control over that! The very act of loving inherently involves the discomfort of vulnerability. When my friend and I had first reconnected after seeing the plethora of swans, I spontaneously blurted out that I would be honoured to have my heartbroken by him. In that moment, I truly felt the gratitude and the rare gift of loving someone even briefly, of feeling *those* feelings, the ones that mean I am vulnerable and open to the pains involved in loving.

It is a choice at midlife, when we are no longer naïve to the pains of loving, to open ourselves again to that vulnerability. I am self-protective and take zinc, I tell myself all sorts of good reasons why loving isn't a good idea, such as how it will disrupt my life as a mother and my vocation, my two primary loves. That "I" is the conscious ego, trying to protect me, and I'm thankful for it for doing a good job. But my heart and soul want to be brave and experience life fully, and that means being honoured to have my heartbroken. Nevertheless, it was not my choice to make, Eros had left our dyad and our loving friendship remained. This too is soul-making or *of soul's making*. Psyche had only intended for this to be a fleeting experience of loving. It remains a beautiful mystery for which I am grateful.

Such experiences and encounters are exquisite, maybe they are not meant to be caught and kept, but enjoyed just as they are, and when it comes time to release them, to let them gently glide back into the water. I have come to love the process of loving: the vulnerable bid for connection, the rejections, the excited potential, the intimacy, the heart swelling, the disappointments, the fading or disappearing—not seeking the heady rush of falling in and out of love pursuing the king in the external world, but appreciating the gift of being human and feeling all the emotions as they arise in my life. My life's journey has not been one of long-term romantic love, I believe that is why I investigate it. At the conclusion of this work, I find there is a joyful acceptance of what is. I value my freedom, son, home, work, writing, being engaged with Psyche, Eros, Aphrodite, and the archetypes, nature, and many friends. What I do have is a beautiful, full, loving life, which I love. It is unexpected, and not what I dreamt of for myself in terms of companionship, but there is peace in the acceptance. I've had stages of ambiguous grief about the absence of companionship. I expect I'll probably have more of those waves, and, at the same time, I am grateful for the abundance of love and soul in my life. Loving is so essential to living. What a blessing to share these moments of beauty and aliveness—even grief becomes beautiful when it is flooded with glistening rays of gratitude.

In conclusion, living a soulful life embraces and celebrates our humanness and intimate relationships and their messy entanglements—it is not seeking to transcend to spiritual heights or escape the confines of the body. It is a way to live in this world and celebrate each glorious moment with its monotony, pain, joy, and pleasure. It is essential to recognize that the unconscious is a codetermining factor along with consciousness and that, with conscious will alone, it is futile to attempt to force or control anything—especially something as archetypal as love. The qualities of receptivity, patience, and acceptance all make the transition from one conscious attitude to another smoother. To live a meaningful, purposeful, rich life, follow what you love and what you are drawn to: soul always follows love and love always follows soul.

Afterword

Upon completing the first draft of this book, I had an interview about the topic with a Jungian colleague. At the end of the interview, he asked how I felt about it. I realized it was the first time I had spoken aloud about the content and shared that with him. He kindly replied, "oh so this is a precious vulnerable moment; like seeing the first baby photos." We come full circle to the baby girl born at the beginning of the writing and now her baby photos are out in the world through the first utterances of her content and nature. Creative works are not so different from romantic love, they are living entities that we can fall in love with and nurture into the world. In fact, the feelings are even the same. Wherever Psyche and Eros calls us, go on dates with them to see where it will go. Not all meetings will grow into loving relationships, but for the ones that do, they are the juicy stuff of life.

References

Apuleius. (1998). *The golden ass.* New York, NY: Penguin.

Bolen, J. S. (1984). *Goddesses in everywoman: Powerful archetypes in women's lives.* New York, NY: Harper Perennial.

Carotenuto, A. (1989). *Eros and pathos: Shades of love and suffering.* Toronto, Canada: Inner City Books.

Castillejo, I. C. (1973). *Knowing woman: A feminine psychology.* Boston, MA: Shambhala.

Chödrön, P. (2000). *When things fall apart.* Boston, MA: Shambhala.

Douglas, C. (1990). *The woman in the mirror: Analytical psychology and the feminine.* Lincoln, NE: iUniverse.

Downing, C. (1981). *The goddess: Mythological images of the feminine.* Lincoln, NE: iUniverse.

Downing, C. (1989). *Myths and mysteries of same-sex love.* New York, NY: Continuum.

Downing, C. (Ed.) (1991). *Mirrors of the self: Archetypal images that shape your life.* Los Angeles, CA: Jeremy P. Tarcher.

Gibran, K. (1923). *The prophet.* London, England: Wordsworth Editions.

Harding, M. E. (1970). *The way of all women.* Boston, MA: Shambhala.

Hillman, J. (1972). *The myth of analysis*. New York, NY: North-western University Press.

Hillman, J. (1975). *Re-visioning psychology*. New York, NY: Harper & Row.

Hillman, J. (1989). *A blue fire*. New York, NY: Harper & Row.

Hillman, J. (2007b). *Mythic figures*. Putnam, CT: Spring.

Hillman, J., & Pozzo, L. (1983). Loving. In *Inter views: Conversations with Laura Pozzo on psychotherapy, biography, love, soul, dreams, work, imagination, and the state of the culture* (pp. 177-194). New York, NY: Harper & Row.

Hollis, J. (1998). *The Eden project: In search of the magical other*. Toronto, Canada: Inner City Books.

Hooks, B. (2002). *Communion: The female search for love*. New York, NY: HarperCollins.

Johnson, R. A. (1983). *We: Understanding the psychology of romantic love*. New York, NY: HarperCollins.

Johnson, R. A. (1989). *She: Understanding feminine psychology*. New York, NY: HarperCollins.

Jung, C. G. (1969). *Aion*. (R. F. C. Hull, Trans.). In H. Read et al. (Series Eds.), *The collected works of C. G. Jung* (Vol. 9ii, pp. 23-71). Princeton, NJ: Princeton University Press. (Original work published 1959)

Jung, C. G. (1969). The transcendent function. In R. F. C. Hull (Trans.), *The collected works of C. G. Jung* (Vol. 8, pp. 67-91). Princeton, NJ: Princeton University Press. (Original work published in 1929)

Jung, C. G. (1997). Patterns of behavior and archetypes. In R. F. C. Hull (Trans.), *The collected works of C. G. Jung* (Vol. 8, pp. 200-217). Princeton, NJ: Princeton University Press. (Original work published 1937)

Jung, C. G. (2010). *Answer to Job.* Princeton, NJ: Princeton University Press. (Original work published 1958)

Moore, T. (1994). *Soul mates: Honoring the mysteries of love and relationship.* New York, NY: HarperCollins.

Neumann, E. (1956). *Amor and Psyche: The psychic development of the feminine.* New York, NY: Princeton University Press.

Rumi (1995). *The essential Rumi* (C. Barks, Trans.). New York, NY: HarperOne.

Spiegelman, M., & Miyuki, M. (1985). *Buddhism and Jungian psychology.* Phoenix, AZ: Falcon Press.

von Franz, M.-L. (1980a). *Alchemy: An introduction to the symbolism and the psychology.* Toronto, Canada: Inner City Books.

von Franz, M.-L. (1980b). *The psychological meaning of redemption motifs in fairytales.* Toronto, Canada: Inner City Books.

von Franz, M.-L. (1995). *Projection and re-collection in Jungian psychology: Reflections of the soul.* Chicago, IL: Open Court.

von Franz, M.-L. (1999). *The cat: A tale of feminine redemption.* Toronto, Canada: Inner City Books.

von Franz, M.-L. (2001). *Golden ass of Apuleius: The liberation of the feminine in man.* Boston, MA: Shambhala.

Wilhelm, R. (1931). *The secret of the golden flower: A Chinese book of life.* San Diego, CA: Book Tree.

Woodman, M. (1982). *Addicted to perfection: The still unravished bride.* Toronto, Canada: Inner City Books.

Woodman, M. (1985). *The pregnant virgin: A process of psychological transformation.* Toronto, Canada: Inner City Books.

Woodman, M. (1990). *The ravaged bridegroom: Masculinity in women.* Toronto, Canada: Inner City Books.

Woodman, M. (1993). *Conscious femininity: Interviews with Marion Woodman.* Toronto, Canada: Inner City Books.

CPSIA information can be obtained
at www.ICGtesting.com
Printed in the USA
LVHW021114210422
716756LV00001B/1

9 781685 030391